ALA-APA Salary Survey: Librarian—Public and Academic

A Survey of Library Positions Requiring an ALA-Accredited Master's Degree

2012

Lorelle Swader
Project Director

ALA-APA Survey Report

American Library Association-Allied Professional Association: the Organization for the Advancement of Library Employees

American Library Association, Office for Research and Statistics

ISBN-10: 0-8389-8616-1
ISBN-13: 978-0-8389-8616-5

Printed in the United States of America

Table of Contents

Acknowledgments

Thanks are due to the many respondents who completed the 2012 Librarian Salary Survey questionnaire. Without their cooperation, this report would not be possible. We are grateful for the responses from new participants as we continue to fulfill our goal to gather and report state level data. And we are indebted to the staff at larger public and academic libraries that participate every year without fail. Association of Research Libraries (ARL) members were willing, as they have since 1991, to share their data with us, as described in Appendix B. We thank Martha Kyrillidou, Director for ARL Statistics and Service Quality Programs, for her support and coordination of this aspect of the

project. The survey was conducted by Counting Opinions (SQUIRE) Ltd of Toronto, Canada. Lindsay Thompson, Survey Manager, executed the survey with professionalism and a continued commitment to improve the experience for participants, with the help of Karen Kupiec, Customer Support Specialist. The Association managed the mailings, processed the returns and analyzed the results. Finally, thanks are due to all in the library community who complete the survey, purchase the survey in print or by subscribing to the Library Salary Database, and use the survey for professional and personal research. We appreciate Angela Hanshaw, who formatted this edition, as she has so ably for four years.

Introduction

The American Library Association-Allied Professional Association: the Organization for Advancement of Library Employees (ALA-APA) has conducted a national survey of librarian salaries in partnership with the American Library Association Office for Research and Statistics (ORS) for seven years. The survey, previously known as the ALA Survey of Librarian Salaries, was conducted periodically from 1982 to 2004 to gather salaries of full-time professionals in academic and public libraries.

We continue to provide this survey to ensure that librarians, the people who hire them and interested others will have accurate data about the salaries paid to librarians in a particular position and working in a particular type of library. This survey included smaller public libraries (serving less than 10,000)—of our nation's 9,249 total public library systems, almost 60 percent serve populations less than 10,000. Of all public libraries, 22 percent have the equivalent of two full-time staff persons with an ALA-accredited Master's degree. There are 4,076 academic libraries nationwide, 37 percent of which have two or more ALA-MLS staff. The survey continues to gather and report salary data at the state-level as well as regionally.

The survey was conducted by the ALA-APA in consultation with ORS. Counting Opinions (SQUIRE), Ltd. of Toronto, Canada prepared the web-based surveys, answered respondent questions and performed the processing and computer analysis of the survey responses.

Details of the Librarian Salary Survey:

- It includes salaries for six positions:
  - Director/Dean/Chief Officer
  - Deputy/Associate/Assistant Director
  - Department Head/Branch Manager/ Coordinator/Senior Manager
  - Manager/Supervisor of Support Staff
  - Librarian Who Does Not Supervise
  - Beginning Librarian
- It was based on a survey of libraries with at least two staff members with an ALA-accredited Master's degree. See Appendix B for more information.
- Data for the nation is stratified into four geographic areas, as well as by state: North Atlantic, Great Lakes & Plains, Southeast and West & Southwest. See Appendix B for a list of states included in each region.
- It shows the first quartile, median and third quartile for salaries paid in each type/size of library in addition to the mean and range (minimum and maximum) for each position reported.

The annual salary survey includes "Supplementary Questions" to gather information on an issue related to library personnel. For 2011, the respondents were asked to answer the following questions:

1. Has the current economic downturn affected your library's spending on recruitment? Select all that apply, and the estimated percentage change.
   - Spending on recruitment
     - Increased: 1–3%, 4–6%, 7–10%, more than 10%
     - Decreased: 1–3%, 4–6%, 7–10%, more than 10%
   - Spending on professional development for staff
     - Increased: 1–3%, 4–6%, 7–10%, more than 10%
     - Decreased: 1–3%, 4–6%, 7–10%, more than 10%
2. Has the current economic downturn affected your library's recruitment efforts in any of the following ways? Select all that apply.
   - Recruiting for vacancies only (Y/N/Don't Know)
   - Recruiting for newly formed positions (Y/N/ Don't Know)
   - Recruiting in all departments (Y/N/Don't Know)
   - Recruiting in some departments, but not all departments (Y/N/Don't Know)
3. Has the current economic downturn resulted in changes in library services? Mark all that apply.
   - Increase of library services (Y/N/Don't Know)
   - Decrease of library services (Y/N/Don't Know)

- Library services increased to particular audiences (Y/N/Don't Know)
- Library services decreased to particular audiences (Y/N/Don't Know)

4. Do any librarian staff positions require bilingual or multi-lingual skills? (Y/N/Don't Know)

5. Are bilingual or multi-lingual skills required for any of the following library services? Mark all that apply.
   - Collection development
   - Liaison to non-English speaking patrons
   - Literacy or library skills training for library patrons
   - Reference assistance
   - Technology training for library patrons
   - Provide Public Programs

6. Which of your library's employees are covered by a collective bargaining agreement?
   - Librarians
   - Other Professional Staff
   - Support Staff

7. Which compensation strategies do you use in your current pay system?
   - Cost of Living Allowances (COLA)
   - Scale plus Cost of Living Allowances (COLA)

- Cash Incentives
- Bonuses (variable Pay)
- Broadbanding
- Job-based or Skill-based Pay
- Merit Pay
- Other Pay Options (Please list)

8. What additional forms of compensation do you provide?
   - Award Programs
   - Compensatory Times
   - Conference Attendance
   - Membership Dues
   - Sabbaticals
   - Team-based Pay
   - Other (please list)

Results of the supplemental questions and analyses of the data are fully reported separately in issues of the ALA-APA monthly newsletter, Library Worklife: HR E-News for Today's Leaders, http://ala-apa.org/newsletter/past-issues/, as well as on the ALA Office for Research and Statistics' web site, www.ala.org/ala/aboutala/offices/ors/index.cfm#Reports.

Results

The survey questionnaire was mailed to a stratified random sample of 1,669 public and academic libraries, including a sample of the membership of the Association of Research Libraries (ARL). The samples were drawn from the 2010 National Center for Education Statistics (NCES) data files *Academic Libraries: 2010* and *Public Library (Public Use) Data File, Fiscal Year 2009*. Surveys were sent to a sample of 1,005 public and 664 academic libraries, using a proportional sampling procedure. Libraries received a letter sent in January 2012 directing them to the complete the survey by using a web site developed by The Management Association of Illinois.

By April 15, 2012 usable responses had been received from 618 libraries (354 public, 264 academic), 37 percent of those sampled. In 2010, the survey had a 35 percent response rate. The response rates since 2004 have fluctuated when respondent follow-up was reduced, and lower since the sample size was increased to collect state-level data and in 2006 and 2007 when both the *ALA-APA Salary Survey: Librarian—Public and Academic (Librarian Salary Survey)* and *ALA-APA Salary Survey: Non-MLS—Public and Academic (Non-MLS Salary Survey)* were issued. See **Complicating Factors** in the **Discussion** section for more details.

The results of this survey are presented on the following pages in six sets of tables for public libraries and six sets of tables for academic libraries. Each set reflects salaries for each position title (see Appendix A for position descriptions). Association of Research Libraries (ARL) member data was included with University data for four positions.

- Director/Dean/Chief Officer—**includes Association of Research Libraries member data (ARL)**
- Deputy/Associate/Assistant Director—**includes ARL**
- Department Head/Branch Manager/ Coordinator/Senior Manager
- Manager/Supervisor of Support Staff
- Librarian Who Does Not Supervise—**includes ARL**
- Beginning Librarian—**includes ARL**

The tables present the number of positions for which salaries were reported (N), the minimum salary and the maximum salary (range), the mean (arithmetic average), first quartile, median and third quartile for each of the four U.S. Census regions and for states. This pattern is repeated for each type and size of library.

Caveats

Caveats should be observed in reading the tables. The intent of the survey is to collect and present a statistically valid report of regional and state-level data for each position and library type. This was not possible for all positions, library types, regions, and states; however, the response rate is adequate for reporting. We received at least one response from a public or academic library in 50 states and the District of Columbia, separating those responses by library class and region reduced the significance of individual library responses.

Responses were received from all states. However, there were no responses from public libraries in Alaska, Delaware, Iowa, North Dakota, and West Virginia, and none from academic libraries in Alaska, Montana, and Wyoming.

Due to increased awareness and reminders from state library data coordinators, state library association staff and ALA state chapter councilors, the response rates were 50 percent or higher for either public or academic libraries in 28 states and for both public and academic libraries in Arizona, Colorado, District of Columbia, Hawaii, Louisiana, Nebraska, Oklahoma, South Dakota and Utah.

Regional and state-level salaries are reported in this survey for each position and by type of library. Individual cases are not presented where there are so few libraries or library systems in a category or state that it would be possible to identify the individual salary, such as in a state where there is one Very

Large public library and one Director. Standard association practices recommend that salaries only be reported when there are three or more responses. These data are not statistically representative because of the response rate, so use caution in reviewing them or reusing them in any way. Table 2 is response rate by library type and shows that very large public libraries had the highest response rate at 58 percent, which was lower than in 2010 (74 percent). Very Small library responses increased from 13 percent in 2010 to 31 percent in 2012.

University and ARL response rates rose from 41 percent in 2010 to 53 percent in 2012. The higher the number of cases (N), the more reliable the results of the sample in providing a true picture of the total population.

Response rates are defined as the percentage of the number of responses received divided by the total number of surveys sent by category. All four regions' Very Large public library response rates were greater than 50 percent. This is important to consider when evaluating salaries for each position by library type, region and state. By region, for example, 39 surveys were sent to Very Large public

Table 1. Response Rate by State and Library Type

State	Invited Sample (No.)		Participants (No.)		Response Rate (%)	
	Public	Academic	Public	Academic	Public	Academic
AL	11	18	2	8	18	44
AK	4	2	0	0	0	0
AZ	8	7	5	4	63	57
AR	11	8	2	3	18	38
CA	78	27	33	14	42	52
CO	19	11	10	7	53	64
CT	32	7	9	1	28	14
DE	3	3	0	1	0	33
DC	1	3	1	2	100	67
FL	37	25	17	7	46	28
GA	30	18	8	7	27	39
HI	1	4	1	2	100	50
ID	6	1	2	1	33	100
IL	54	24	20	10	37	42
IN	37	17	9	8	24	47
IA	14	10	6	5	43	50
KS	10	10	3	5	30	50
KY	8	10	3	4	38	40
LA	8	11	4	8	50	73
ME	15	6	4	3	27	50
MD	10	16	6	7	60	44
MA	48	23	24	9	50	39
MI	42	17	7	5	17	29
MN	14	10	1	4	7	40
MS	12	11	5	3	42	27
MO	12	21	7	9	58	43
MT	3	2	2	0	67	0
NE	4	7	3	5	75	71
NV	5	3	3	1	60	33
NH	10	6	1	1	10	17
NJ	71	18	20	1	28	6
NM	6	4	2	3	33	75
NY	84	53	15	20	18	38
NC	19	24	5	9	26	38
ND	1	5	0	3	0	60
OH	40	22	20	8	50	36
OK	7	9	4	5	57	56
OR	14	10	6	3	43	30
PA	51	33	17	13	33	39
RI	9	6	4	2	44	33
SC	15	19	6	7	40	37

Table 1. Response Rate by State and Library Type continued

State	Invited Sample (No.)		Participants (No.)		Response Rate (%)	
	Public	Academic	Public	Academic	Public	Academic
SD	1	2	1	1	100	50
TN	10	18	5	7	50	39
TX	48	30	20	12	42	40
UT	3	6	2	4	67	67
VT	4	7	3	1	75	14
VA	16	20	6	6	38	30
WA	11	17	5	9	45	53
WV	4	7	0	4	0	57
WI	40	13	12	2	30	15
WY	4	3	3	0	75	0
Total	1,005	664	354	264	35	40

Table 2. Response Rate by Library Type

	Responding Libraries (No.)	Libraries Invited to Participate (No.)	Response Rate (%)
Very Small Public	22	72	31
Small Public	61	236	26
Medium Public	118	392	30
Large Public	105	222	47
Very Large Public	48	83	58
2-Year College	79	195	41
4-Year College	61	237	26
ARL & University	124	232	53
Total	618	1,669	37

libraries in the West & Southwest region and 21 responded (21/39 = 54 percent). Another caveat is that when the mean and the median are not close together, the mean is being influenced by some unusual values. When the mean is much higher than the median, there are several very high salaries. When the mean is much lower than the median, there are several very low salaries. The following examples illustrate how to interpret the tables:

Public

On the first page of the public library tables, there were 11 Director salaries reported by Very Small public libraries from the North Atlantic region. The minimum salary for the

range reported for this position in this region was $70,948 and the maximum was $88,052. When all of the salaries were added together and the result was divided by the total number (11), the average or mean salary was 78,580. When all 19 of the Director salaries for all regions were arrayed from low to high, 25 percent fell below $51,147 (Q1), 50 percent fell at or below $72,000 (median) and 75 percent fell below $93,337 (Q3). The mean overall of $70,870 and median of $72,000 were $1,330 apart, meaning that Directors in the bottom 50 percent pulled the average down by more than $1,000. State-level data for Directors of Very Small public libraries follows in the table below. A final set of cumulative Regional- and State-level data tables for Directors of all public libraries follows the five sets of tables for each size of public library.

Academic

On the first page of the academic library tables, there were eight Director salaries reported by Two-Year College Libraries from the North Atlantic region. The minimum salary for the range reported for this position in this region was $57,766 and the maximum was $107,461. When all of the salaries were added together and the result was divided by the total number (8), the average or mean salary was $73,239. When all 63 of the Director salaries for all regions were arrayed from low to high, 25 percent of Director salaries fell below $57,771 (Q1), 50 percent fell at or below $65,145 (median) and 75 percent fell below $76,024 (Q3). The mean overall of $67,382 and median of $65,145 were $2,237 apart, indicating that Directors in the top 50 percent earned higher salaries, bringing up the overall average. State-level data for Directors of Two-Year college libraries follows in the table below. A final set of cumulative Regional- and State-level data tables for Directors of all academic libraries follows the three sets of tables for each type of academic library.

DIRECTOR/DEAN/CHIEF OFFICER

Chief officer of the library or library system.

Very Small Public Library (serving a population of less than 10,000)

Regional Data

	Min	Q1	Mean	Median	Q3	Max	N
Great Lakes & Plains	50,147	50,182	61,232	50,722	93,337	93,337	8
North Atlantic	70,948	72,000	78,580	79,000	88,052	88,052	11
ALL REGIONS	50,147	51,251	70,870	72,000	93,337	93,337	19

State Data

	Min	Q1	Mean	Median	Q3	Max	N
CT	72,000	72,000	72,000	72,000	72,000	72,000	1
IA	50,147	50,147	50,147	50,147	50,147	50,147	1
IL	50,350	66,625	69,147	67,425	68,000	93,337	5
MA	65,000	69,590	74,873	73,220	78,502	88,052	4
NE	51,251	51,251	51,251	51,251	51,251	51,251	1
NJ	68,450	72,680	75,415	75,155	77,890	82,900	4
NY	79,000	79,000	79,000	79,000	79,000	79,000	1
OH	50,193	50,193	50,193	50,193	50,193	50,193	1
VT	70,948	70,948	70,948	70,948	70,948	70,948	1

DIRECTOR/DEAN/CHIEF OFFICER—CONTINUED

Small Public Library (serving a population of 10,000 to 24,999)

Regional Data

	Min	Q1	Mean	Median	Q3	Max	N
Great Lakes & Plains	45,020	57,651	69,383	70,073	95,000	95,000	13
North Atlantic	54,075	60,788	79,842	72,271	131,000	131,000	36
Southeast	69,769	69,769	69,769	69,769	69,769	69,769	1
West & Southwest	51,150	78,000	89,447	85,686	134,511	134,511	7
ALL REGIONS	45,020	60,788	78,661	72,271	134,511	134,511	57

State Data

	Min	Q1	Mean	Median	Q3	Max	N
CA	122,720	125,668	128,616	128,616	131,563	134,511	2
CT	60,000	65,830	67,977	71,660	71,966	72,271	3
GA	69,769	69,769	69,769	69,769	69,769	69,769	1
IA	69,700	69,700	69,700	69,700	69,700	69,700	1
IL	52,000	54,500	67,414	56,000	79,568	95,000	5
KS	45,020	45,020	45,020	45,020	45,020	45,020	1
MA	65,720	68,697	76,592	74,255	85,757	89,534	8

ME	54,075	54,075	54,075	54,075	54,075	54,075	1
MI	53,634	53,634	53,634	53,634	53,634	53,634	1
NH	59,800	59,800	59,800	59,800	59,800	59,800	1
NJ	57,500	80,179	88,211	88,961	101,000	106,625	8
NY	60,000	67,060	96,541	105,000	115,015	131,000	8
OH	54,511	61,508	68,506	68,506	75,503	82,500	2
OK	78,000	78,000	78,000	78,000	78,000	78,000	1
OR	51,150	51,150	51,150	51,150	51,150	51,150	1
PA	31,810	43,815	52,205	49,440	67,000	68,959	5
RI	60,788	60,788	60,788	60,788	60,788	60,788	1
TX	73,165	79,346	85,527	85,527	91,708	97,889	2
VT	75,524	75,524	75,524	75,524	75,524	75,524	1
WA	85,686	85,686	85,686	85,686	85,686	85,686	1
WI	55,137	61,554	64,517	67,970	69,208	70,445	3

DIRECTOR/DEAN/CHIEF OFFICER—CONTINUED

Medium Public Library (serving a population of 25,000 to 99,999)

Regional Data

	Min	Q1	Mean	Median	Q3	Max	N
Great Lakes & Plains	69,557	89,245	104,935	106,766	142,768	142,768	37
North Atlantic	85,000	95,596	114,151	100,000	152,363	152,363	35
Southeast	58,494	65,000	78,067	74,277	106,090	106,090	13
West & Southwest	67,840	77,916	95,883	90,000	155,013	155,013	28
ALL REGIONS	58,494	77,812	96,819	96,284	155,013	155,013	113

State Data

	Min	Q1	Mean	Median	Q3	Max	N
AL	103,812	103,812	103,812	103,812	103,812	103,812	1
AR	85,000	85,000	85,000	85,000	85,000	85,000	1
CA	74,106	99,145	121,086	125,484	147,354	155,013	7
CO	90,000	91,701	94,456	93,392	96,147	101,041	4
CT	74,176	92,007	97,523	99,523	101,647	120,062	6
FL	74,277	74,277	74,277	74,277	74,277	74,277	1
IA	80,000	90,575	102,372	101,150	113,558	125,965	3
ID	80,000	80,000	80,000	80,000	80,000	80,000	1
IL	78,516	98,857	108,810	105,831	121,736	142,768	10
IN	64,496	64,799	71,529	70,310	77,039	81,000	4
KY	58,814	58,814	58,814	58,814	58,814	58,814	1
LA	72,530	72,530	72,530	72,530	72,530	72,530	1
MA	49,559	66,303	75,183	75,499	86,167	96,284	7
ME	85,000	85,000	85,000	85,000	85,000	85,000	1
MI	58,900	69,892	81,564	78,180	89,852	110,997	4
MO	64,000	65,176	66,636	66,351	67,954	69,557	3
MS	42,000	46,124	50,247	50,247	54,371	58,494	2

MT	63,630	65,689	67,747	67,747	69,806	71,864	2
NJ	75,000	83,561	100,719	87,757	104,916	152,363	4
NM	78,227	78,227	78,227	78,227	78,227	78,227	1
NV	100,000	100,000	100,000	100,000	100,000	100,000	1
NY	57,863	100,716	111,427	118,700	129,411	150,444	4
OH	59,480	80,499	89,398	92,477	104,630	106,766	6
OK	67,840	67,840	67,840	67,840	67,840	67,840	1
OR	77,812	77,812	77,812	77,812	77,812	77,812	1
PA	47,476	59,731	68,577	65,732	72,100	100,000	10
RI	67,918	69,959	78,275	72,000	83,454	94,907	3
SC	43,722	47,861	58,102	52,000	65,292	78,584	3
TN	65,000	65,000	65,000	65,000	65,000	65,000	1
TX	46,972	59,001	72,476	59,636	90,472	113,012	8
VA	48,056	62,565	77,073	77,073	91,582	106,090	2
WI	73,949	74,747	82,155	75,670	89,243	97,490	7
WY	53,596	68,702	83,808	83,808	98,914	114,020	2

DIRECTOR/DEAN/CHIEF OFFICER—CONTINUED

Large Public Library (serving a population of 100,000 to 499,999)

Regional Data

	Min	Q1	Mean	Median	Q3	Max	N
Great Lakes & Plains	80,060	112,716	124,050	127,275	165,000	165,000	20
North Atlantic	98,921	106,574	126,862	125,857	170,000	170,000	12
Southeast	57,553	90,859	96,766	100,802	122,235	122,235	29
West & Southwest	72,000	96,940	112,983	110,000	179,916	179,916	33
ALL REGIONS	57,553	98,125	113,275	110,000	179,916	179,916	94

State Data

	Min	Q1	Mean	Median	Q3	Max	N
AR	75,898	75,898	75,898	75,898	75,898	75,898	1
AZ	96,117	96,117	96,117	96,117	96,117	96,117	1
CA	80,929	108,720	130,721	134,821	144,997	179,916	13
CO	92,500	98,271	104,614	104,041	110,671	117,300	3
CT	98,921	98,921	98,921	98,921	98,921	98,921	1
FL	71,000	79,877	86,961	87,505	91,940	105,000	6
GA	55,111	76,651	79,413	81,197	103,711	100,145	4
ID	96,940	96,940	96,940	96,940	96,940	96,940	1
IN	88,987	97,772	110,510	102,854	115,592	147,347	4
KS	89,984	99,875	109,767	109,767	119,658	129,549	2
KY	101,459	101,459	101,459	101,459	101,459	101,459	1
LA	69,822	75,725	81,629	81,629	87,532	93,435	2
MA	70,226	83,793	97,360	97,360	110,927	124,494	2
MD	120,000	124,984	129,968	129,968	134,952	139,936	2
MI	115,128	117,596	120,064	120,064	122,532	125,000	2

MO	80,060	80,060	80,060	80,060	80,060	80,060	1
MS	51,916	66,927	74,618	81,937	85,969	90,000	3
NC	65,333	71,122	84,052	84,262	97,192	102,350	4
NE	94,205	103,088	111,971	111,971	120,854	129,737	2
NJ	93,000	99,448	108,705	105,895	116,558	127,220	3
NV	110,045	110,045	110,045	110,045	110,045	110,045	1
NY	100,600	100,600	100,600	100,600	100,600	100,600	1
OH	75,036	88,386	107,846	93,704	122,205	165,000	7
OR	86,890	93,864	99,243	100,838	105,419	110,000	3
PA	41,000	55,288	93,525	69,576	119,788	170,000	3
SC	70,299	76,597	90,925	82,894	101,238	119,582	3
SD	117,579	117,579	117,579	117,579	117,579	117,579	1
TN	57,553	57,553	57,553	57,553	57,553	57,553	1
TX	77,250	90,636	96,921	94,441	101,141	127,058	8
UT	72,000	72,000	72,000	72,000	72,000	72,000	1
VA	75,000	80,202	99,914	101,211	120,923	122,235	4
WA	107,472	107,472	107,472	107,472	107,472	107,472	1
WI	98,125	98,125	98,125	98,125	98,125	98,125	1

DIRECTOR/DEAN/CHIEF OFFICER—CONTINUED

Very Large Public Library (serving a population of 500,000 or more)

Regional Data

	Min	Q1	Mean	Median	Q3	Max	N
Great Lakes & Plains	125,460	139,551	150,394	146,351	183,413	183,413	9
North Atlantic	175,000	181,500	184,333	188,000	190,000	190,000	6
Southeast	88,000	125,000	138,632	137,667	191,195	191,195	11
West & Southwest	114,000	137,175	152,260	144,045	212,345	212,345	23
ALL REGIONS	88,000	137,333	153,891	147,180	212,345	212,345	49

State Data

	Min	Q1	Mean	Median	Q3	Max	N
AZ	129,501	132,353	135,206	135,206	138,058	140,910	2
CA	116,743	147,525	164,486	158,736	187,109	212,345	6
CO	81,245	108,420	117,947	135,595	136,298	137,000	3
DC	188,000	188,000	188,000	188,000	188,000	188,000	1
FL	95,743	120,510	142,960	136,092	171,514	191,195	6
GA	94,260	107,837	117,669	121,414	129,374	137,333	3
HI	114,000	114,000	114,000	114,000	114,000	114,000	1
MA	175,000	175,000	175,000	175,000	175,000	175,000	1
MD	135,000	137,063	162,874	163,248	189,060	190,000	4
MN	144,248	144,248	144,248	144,248	144,248	144,248	1
MO	125,000	130,864	136,727	136,727	142,591	148,454	2
NC	138,000	138,000	138,000	138,000	138,000	138,000	1
NV	166,254	166,254	166,254	166,254	166,254	166,254	1

OH	95,000	96,425	136,860	134,514	174,949	183,413	5
OK	140,000	151,582	163,163	163,163	174,745	186,326	2
OR	137,700	137,700	137,700	137,700	137,700	137,700	1
TN	88,000	88,000	88,000	88,000	88,000	88,000	1
TX	122,080	128,355	134,630	134,630	140,905	147,180	2
UT	87,192	95,058	102,924	102,924	110,790	118,656	2
WA	146,740	148,488	153,067	150,235	156,231	162,227	3
WI	125,460	125,460	125,460	125,460	125,460	125,460	1

DIRECTOR/DEAN/CHIEF OFFICER—CONTINUED
ALL PUBLIC LIBRARIES

Regional Data

	Min	Q1	Mean	Median	Q3	Max	N
Great Lakes & Plains	45,020	69,629	92,659	89,984	107,973	183,413	88
North Atlantic	31,810	67,918	89,379	80,260	101,019	190,000	98
Southeast	42,000	70,180	89,226	83,947	102,716	191,195	56
West & Southwest	46,972	86,966	111,266	105,757	137,525	212,345	90
ALL REGIONS	31,810	71,255	96,187	90,018	115,282	212,345	332

State Data

	Min	Q1	Mean	Median	Q3	Max	N
AL	103,812	103,812	103,812	103,812	103,812	103,812	1
AR	85,000	85,000	85,000	85,000	85,000	85,000	1
AZ	96,117	112,809	122,176	129,501	135,206	140,910	3
CA	74,106	114,737	135,397	137,269	151,838	212,345	28
CO	81,245	92,326	104,551	97,778	113,985	137,000	10
CT	72,000	74,176	92,037	98,027	101,019	120,062	9
DC	188,000	188,000	188,000	188,000	188,000	188,000	1
FL	60,000	76,222	105,697	92,587	125,687	191,195	15
GA	55,111	71,520	92,553	92,275	105,462	137,333	8
HI	114,000	114,000	114,000	114,000	114,000	114,000	1
IA	50,147	77,563	94,848	103,025	114,144	125,965	6
ID	80,000	84,235	88,470	88,470	92,705	96,940	2
IL	50,350	67,225	88,545	91,198	104,156	142,768	20
IN	64,496	73,014	91,020	84,994	101,777	147,347	8
KS	45,020	67,502	88,184	89,984	109,767	129,549	3
KY	58,814	69,475	80,137	80,137	90,798	101,459	2
LA	69,822	71,176	78,596	72,530	82,983	93,435	3
MA	49,559	68,099	82,192	75,409	87,728	175,000	22
MD	120,000	135,688	151,905	138,843	176,544	190,000	6
ME	54,075	61,806	69,538	69,538	77,269	85,000	2
MI	53,634	66,228	88,574	82,804	113,063	125,000	7
MN	144,248	144,248	144,248	144,248	144,248	144,248	1
MO	64,000	67,153	92,237	74,809	113,765	148,454	6

MS	42,000	51,916	64,869	58,494	81,937	90,000	5
MT	63,630	65,689	67,747	67,747	69,806	71,864	2
NC	65,333	73,052	94,841	95,472	102,350	138,000	5
NE	51,251	72,728	91,731	94,205	111,971	129,737	3
NH	59,800	59,800	59,800	59,800	59,800	59,800	1
NJ	57,500	77,661	91,386	88,800	102,000	152,363	19
NM	78,227	78,227	78,227	78,227	78,227	78,227	1
NV	100,000	105,023	125,433	110,045	138,150	166,254	3
NY	57,863	71,113	99,831	105,300	120,550	150,444	14
OH	50,193	81,496	101,298	94,352	105,581	183,413	21
OK	67,840	75,460	118,042	109,000	151,582	186,326	4
OR	51,150	80,082	94,065	93,864	107,710	137,700	6
PA	31,810	49,440	68,164	65,732	69,576	170,000	18
RI	60,788	66,136	73,903	69,959	77,727	94,907	4
SC	43,722	56,575	74,514	74,442	81,817	119,582	6
SD	117,579	117,579	117,579	117,579	117,579	117,579	1
TN	57,553	61,277	70,184	65,000	76,500	88,000	3
TX	46,972	69,937	89,774	92,424	101,141	147,180	20
UT	72,000	79,596	92,616	87,192	102,924	118,656	3
VA	48,056	76,734	92,301	94,013	116,887	122,235	6
VT	70,948	72,092	73,236	73,236	74,380	75,524	2
WA	85,686	107,472	130,472	146,740	150,235	162,227	5
WI	55,137	73,073	82,685	75,335	92,367	125,460	12
WY	53,596	68,702	83,808	83,808	98,914	114,020	2

DEPUTY/ASSOCIATE/ASSISTANT DIRECTOR

Persons who report to the Director and manage major aspects of the library operation (e.g., technical services, public services, collection development, systems/automation).

Very Small Public Library (serving a population of less than 10,000)

Regional Data

	Min	Q1	Mean	Median	Q3	Max	N
Great Lakes & Plains	47,509	47,509	47,509	47,509	47,509	47,509	1
North Atlantic	46,758	51,665	59,358	56,151	63,844	78,374	6
ALL REGIONS	46,758	47,509	56,988	53,301	59,000	78,374	7

State Data

	Min	Q1	Mean	Median	Q3	Max	N
CT	59,000	59,000	59,000	59,000	59,000	59,000	1
IL	47,509	47,509	47,509	47,509	47,509	47,509	1
MA	58,608	60,664	66,567	62,719	70,547	78,374	3
NJ	53,301	53,301	53,301	53,301	53,301	53,301	1
VT	46,758	46,758	46,758	46,758	46,758	46,758	1

DEPUTY/ASSOCIATE/ASSISTANT DIRECTOR—CONTINUED
Small Public Library (serving a population of 10,000 to 24,999)

Regional Data

	Min	Q1	Mean	Median	Q3	Max	N
Great Lakes & Plains	48,630	51,620	57,631	54,609	62,131	69,653	6
North Atlantic	45,250	54,470	60,695	64,320	66,657	71,660	15
Southeast	36,920	39,371	41,823	41,823	44,274	46,725	3
West & Southwest	50,000	52,841	55,681	55,681	58,522	61,362	2
ALL REGIONS	36,920	48,630	56,313	54,609	64,682	71,660	26

State Data

	Min	Q1	Mean	Median	Q3	Max	N
CT	63,957	63,957	63,957	63,957	63,957	63,957	1
FL	30,000	31,730	33,460	33,460	35,190	36,920	2
GA	46,725	46,725	46,725	46,725	46,725	46,725	1
IA	48,630	48,630	48,630	48,630	48,630	48,630	1
IL	38,000	41,500	50,884	45,000	57,327	69,653	3
MA	50,371	57,298	59,397	57,375	64,628	67,315	5
ME	45,250	45,250	45,250	45,250	45,250	45,250	1
NJ	48,000	58,574	63,190	66,550	71,165	71,660	4
OK	50,000	50,000	50,000	50,000	50,000	50,000	1
PA	27,745	28,562	36,143	29,378	40,343	51,307	3
VT	64,682	64,682	64,682	64,682	64,682	64,682	1
WA	61,362	61,362	61,362	61,362	61,362	61,362	1
WI	48,036	49,679	51,323	51,323	52,966	54,609	2

DEPUTY/ASSOCIATE/ASSISTANT DIRECTOR—CONTINUED
Medium Public Library (serving a population of 25,000 to 99,999)

Regional Data

	Min	Q1	Mean	Median	Q3	Max	N
Great Lakes & Plains	52,438	62,959	78,992	80,330	88,924	116,414	32
North Atlantic	70,448	77,214	85,839	78,731	87,348	120,198	29
Southeast	60,000	60,000	71,751	67,378	79,129	92,248	7
West & Southwest	55,765	61,322	84,355	78,064	95,347	137,388	13
ALL REGIONS	52,438	65,224	80,918	78,071	91,124	137,388	81

State Data

	Min	Q1	Mean	Median	Q3	Max	N
AL	74,756	74,756	74,756	74,756	74,756	74,756	2
AR	60,000	60,000	60,000	60,000	60,000	60,000	1
CA	78,900	105,279	114,210	120,276	129,207	137,388	4
CO	66,435	68,033	69,268	69,631	70,685	71,739	3
CT	67,000	71,529	73,499	74,462	76,432	78,071	4

IA	96,554	96,554	96,554	96,554	96,554	96,554	6
IL	37,065	52,551	73,137	73,763	89,190	116,414	11
IN	43,407	48,040	50,194	52,672	53,588	54,503	2
MA	53,722	59,673	64,048	66,011	70,386	70,448	5
MI	50,273	59,997	67,096	69,721	75,507	81,293	3
MO	52,438	52,438	52,438	52,438	52,438	52,438	2
NJ	90,000	90,000	90,000	90,000	90,000	90,000	1
NM	57,850	57,850	57,850	57,850	57,850	57,850	1
NY	48,172	72,433	87,130	91,598	102,540	120,198	7
OH	62,130	64,491	69,770	66,851	73,591	80,330	3
OK	55,765	55,765	55,765	55,765	55,765	55,765	1
PA	40,804	51,652	56,988	56,208	61,701	79,390	8
RI	55,110	56,135	63,066	57,159	67,044	76,928	3
SC	39,171	44,378	49,586	49,586	54,793	60,000	3
TX	53,186	58,082	66,851	62,978	73,684	84,389	3
VA	92,248	92,248	92,248	92,248	92,248	92,248	1
WI	55,621	55,848	60,592	58,646	61,432	71,414	5
WY	99,000	99,000	99,000	99,000	99,000	99,000	1

DEPUTY/ASSOCIATE/ASSISTANT DIRECTOR—CONTINUED

Large Public Library (serving a population of 100,000 to 499,999)

Regional Data

	Min	Q1	Mean	Median	Q3	Max	N
Great Lakes & Plains	64,804	91,104	98,102	96,793	97,610	153,059	34
North Atlantic	74,481	82,469	88,126	84,229	95,257	105,000	23
Southeast	60,000	73,264	78,241	79,559	83,432	97,900	35
West & Southwest	71,820	78,947	88,551	89,700	92,222	110,064	48
ALL REGIONS	60,000	78,357	88,584	87,282	97,153	153,059	140

State Data

	Min	Q1	Mean	Median	Q3	Max	N
AZ	71,043	81,100	84,807	91,156	91,689	92,222	3
CA	73,644	80,951	90,270	90,184	98,456	110,064	15
CO	71,468	71,781	72,093	72,093	72,406	72,718	2
CT	56,401	61,419	67,928	64,601	74,878	82,340	5
FL	43,000	55,952	64,147	67,723	75,300	76,585	6
GA	52,815	56,636	62,991	60,456	68,079	75,702	4
IA	74,870	79,785	85,454	84,700	90,747	96,793	3
IN	55,340	66,773	73,996	71,950	78,917	97,000	5
KS	67,000	75,642	84,283	84,283	92,925	101,566	2
KY	53,000	54,750	56,500	56,500	58,250	60,000	2
LA	58,406	66,952	77,832	77,511	88,390	97,900	5
MA	52,198	59,862	67,526	67,526	75,190	82,854	3
MD	82,494	83,825	93,669	93,591	103,434	105,000	5

MI	78,059	83,346	85,217	88,633	88,797	88,960	3
MO	64,170	74,085	80,064	84,000	88,011	92,021	3
MS	63,000	64,000	64,650	65,000	65,475	65,950	3
NC	50,000	55,999	66,905	63,257	80,275	82,533	7
NE	85,393	88,447	91,502	91,502	94,556	97,610	2
NJ	70,914	77,957	84,796	85,000	91,738	98,475	3
NY	74,481	74,481	74,481	74,481	74,481	74,481	3
OH	54,330	58,219	72,386	62,517	72,280	153,059	12
OR	60,940	66,385	74,157	71,830	80,765	89,700	3
PA	30,000	62,688	66,234	74,666	78,212	85,603	4
SC	51,788	54,795	62,864	61,737	64,503	84,018	6
SD	91,104	91,104	91,104	91,104	91,104	91,104	3
TX	48,558	56,174	64,937	65,510	73,576	78,947	24
VA	59,386	65,349	71,312	71,312	77,274	83,237	2
WA	71,820	71,820	71,820	71,820	71,820	71,820	1
WI	64,804	64,804	64,804	64,804	64,804	64,804	1

DEPUTY/ASSOCIATE/ASSISTANT DIRECTOR—CONTINUED

Very Large Public Library (serving a population of 500,000 or more)

Regional Data

	Min	Q1	Mean	Median	Q3	Max	N
Great Lakes & Plains	97,823	103,532	120,101	119,291	135,860	144,000	17
North Atlantic	100,916	113,986	130,113	126,167	142,294	167,200	18
Southeast	87,727	94,832	111,260	101,937	123,026	144,115	31
West & Southwest	93,072	101,595	124,022	125,288	134,358	164,559	52
ALL REGIONS	87,727	101,427	122,464	124,779	138,996	167,200	118

State Data

	Min	Q1	Mean	Median	Q3	Max	N
AZ	72,779	79,591	86,520	86,403	93,391	100,379	4
CA	74,151	92,714	117,192	122,231	137,142	164,559	25
CO	96,907	98,180	99,454	99,454	100,727	102,000	2
DC	137,599	144,999	152,400	152,400	159,800	167,200	2
FL	70,995	78,578	99,358	87,486	118,476	144,115	14
GA	54,864	58,464	64,717	60,480	66,510	87,727	8
MA	84,371	97,658	102,873	101,786	112,206	118,342	5
MD	88,927	107,500	117,195	124,848	128,799	133,992	7
MN	72,862	86,008	92,483	99,153	102,294	105,435	3
MO	73,002	83,257	99,808	97,563	112,073	133,147	5
NJ	59,969	68,392	82,188	83,933	97,729	100,916	4
NV	153,670	153,670	153,670	153,670	153,670	153,670	1
OH	110,381	111,363	126,845	124,779	143,704	144,000	5
OK	97,782	107,910	112,595	111,012	118,352	127,920	6
TN	62,905	71,142	76,502	74,000	77,368	101,937	9

TX	90,750	101,483	109,248	112,216	118,498	124,779	5
UT	84,264	86,466	88,668	88,668	90,870	93,072	2
WA	107,853	110,925	117,320	120,805	121,222	125,797	7
WI	79,083	86,810	90,809	93,165	97,163	97,823	4

DEPUTY/ASSOCIATE/ASSISTANT DIRECTOR—CONTINUED
ALL PUBLIC LIBRARIES

Regional Data

	Min	Q1	Mean	Median	Q3	Max	N
Great Lakes & Plains	37,065	58,162	77,802	73,026	92,617	153,059	90
North Atlantic	27,745	57,375	76,441	71,199	90,000	167,200	90
Southeast	30,000	59,693	72,572	70,716	80,275	144,115	76
West & Southwest	48,558	71,149	90,413	86,340	109,526	164,559	115
ALL REGIONS	27,745	60,462	80,044	74,722	96,284	167,200	371

State Data

	Min	Q1	Mean	Median	Q3	Max	N
AL	74,756	74,756	74,756	74,756	74,756	74,756	2
AR	60,000	60,000	60,000	60,000	60,000	60,000	1
AZ	71,043	76,185	85,664	88,780	91,956	100,379	7
CA	73,644	86,754	106,852	103,068	130,840	164,559	44
CO	66,435	70,550	78,700	71,739	84,813	102,000	7
CT	56,401	62,688	68,781	67,000	75,382	82,340	11
DC	137,599	144,999	152,400	152,400	159,800	167,200	2
FL	30,000	71,866	83,764	77,493	103,556	144,115	22
GA	46,725	56,232	62,611	60,456	66,510	87,727	13
IA	48,630	74,870	80,309	84,700	96,554	96,793	10
IL	37,065	46,842	66,978	69,653	84,378	116,414	15
IN	43,407	54,045	65,070	61,057	73,692	97,000	7
KS	67,000	75,642	84,283	84,283	92,925	101,566	2
KY	53,000	54,750	56,500	56,500	58,250	60,000	2
LA	58,406	66,952	77,832	77,511	88,390	97,900	5
MA	50,371	57,992	73,805	67,315	83,613	118,342	21
MD	82,494	95,920	108,640	105,000	126,202	133,992	12
ME	45,250	45,250	45,250	45,250	45,250	45,250	1
MI	50,273	71,806	76,157	79,676	86,798	88,960	6
MN	72,862	86,008	92,483	99,153	102,294	105,435	3
MO	52,438	73,002	87,963	84,000	97,563	133,147	10
MS	63,000	64,000	64,650	65,000	65,475	65,950	3
NC	50,000	55,999	66,905	63,257	80,275	82,533	7
NE	85,393	88,447	91,502	91,502	94,556	97,610	2
NJ	48,000	62,099	75,323	71,199	90,000	100,916	13
NM	57,850	57,850	57,850	57,850	57,850	57,850	1
NV	153,670	153,670	153,670	153,670	153,670	153,670	1

	Min	Q1	Mean	Median	Q3	Max	N
NY	48,172	73,409	85,549	83,136	101,460	120,198	10
OH	54,330	62,130	87,942	72,280	111,363	153,059	20
OK	50,000	76,774	95,534	107,910	114,682	127,920	8
OR	60,940	66,385	74,157	71,830	80,765	89,700	3
PA	27,745	43,347	55,285	55,302	67,969	85,603	15
RI	55,110	56,135	63,066	57,159	67,044	76,928	3
SC	39,171	52,537	59,545	60,412	63,268	84,018	9
SD	91,104	91,104	91,104	91,104	91,104	91,104	3
TN	62,905	71,142	76,502	74,000	77,368	101,937	9
TX	48,558	57,993	69,890	67,951	76,115	124,779	32
UT	84,264	86,466	88,668	88,668	90,870	93,072	2
VA	59,386	71,312	78,290	83,237	87,743	92,248	3
VT	46,758	51,239	55,720	55,720	60,201	64,682	2
WA	61,362	89,837	102,826	110,925	121,014	125,797	9
WI	48,036	55,791	69,470	63,118	81,659	97,823	12
WY	99,000	99,000	99,000	99,000	99,000	99,000	1

DEPARTMENT HEAD/COORDINATOR/SENIOR MANAGER

Persons who supervise one or more professional librarians.

Very Small Public Library (serving a population of less than 10,000)

Regional Data

	Min	Q1	Mean	Median	Q3	Max	N
Great Lakes & Plains	80,550	80,550	80,550	80,550	80,550	80,550	4
North Atlantic	38,452	38,702	47,045	38,952	63,730	63,730	6
ALL REGIONS	38,452	38,827	55,421	51,341	80,550	80,550	10

State Data

	Min	Q1	Mean	Median	Q3	Max	N
IL	33,495	38,605	55,584	54,146	71,125	80,550	4
MA	38,220	44,598	50,975	50,975	57,353	63,730	2
ME	38,452	38,452	38,452	38,452	38,452	38,452	1
NJ	28,344	30,996	33,648	33,648	36,300	38,952	2

DEPARTMENT HEAD/COORDINATOR/SENIOR MANAGER—CONTINUED

Small Public Library (serving a population of 10,000 to 24,999)

Regional Data

	Min	Q1	Mean	Median	Q3	Max	N
Great Lakes & Plains	38,948	51,863	56,620	64,778	66,133	66,133	8
North Atlantic	39,520	49,380	64,709	66,831	97,968	97,968	35
Southeast	36,000	36,000	36,000	36,000	36,000	36,000	4
West & Southwest	79,144	79,144	79,144	79,144	79,144	79,144	1
ALL REGIONS	36,000	41,985	60,855	65,456	97,968	97,968	48

State Data

	Min	Q1	Mean	Median	Q3	Max	N
CA	79,144	79,144	79,144	79,144	79,144	79,144	1
FL	36,000	36,000	36,000	36,000	36,000	36,000	4
IL	38,578	46,866	51,146	50,614	54,894	64,778	4
MA	40,052	46,361	52,930	51,971	57,960	69,844	8
NH	37,856	38,272	38,688	38,688	39,104	39,520	3
NJ	50,000	54,327	58,918	59,530	63,706	66,831	9
NY	55,283	58,471	70,626	62,892	82,211	97,968	12
OH	62,983	63,771	64,558	64,558	65,346	66,133	2
PA	31,531	39,924	43,076	48,316	48,848	49,380	3
WI	38,948	38,948	38,948	38,948	38,948	38,948	2

DEPARTMENT HEAD/COORDINATOR/SENIOR MANAGER—CONTINUED

Medium Public Library (serving a population of 25,000 to 99,999)

Regional Data

	Min	Q1	Mean	Median	Q3	Max	N
Great Lakes & Plains	41,744	56,233	67,177	64,865	104,687	104,687	52
North Atlantic	27,488	42,268	54,306	47,399	98,718	98,718	90
Southeast	48,173	51,923	67,549	60,215	107,182	107,182	31
West & Southwest	41,060	57,800	60,376	62,996	72,352	72,352	68
ALL REGIONS	27,488	49,087	61,977	60,393	107,182	107,182	241

State Data

	Min	Q1	Mean	Median	Q3	Max	N
AL	54,905	54,905	54,905	54,905	54,905	54,905	3
AR	41,744	41,744	41,744	41,744	41,744	41,744	1
CA	53,804	71,006	81,330	85,470	93,250	104,687	21
CO	56,139	56,351	57,658	57,139	58,446	60,216	4
CT	61,661	63,768	66,759	65,647	70,238	71,995	21
IA	69,514	69,514	69,514	69,514	69,514	69,514	2
IL	48,692	56,419	67,107	63,578	74,540	98,718	29
IN	31,200	32,365	38,185	40,676	41,243	45,440	15
LA	46,550	46,795	47,039	47,039	47,284	47,528	2
MA	24,114	38,588	46,264	48,841	54,929	60,393	20
ME	40,924	40,924	44,097	44,097	47,270	47,270	14
MI	45,020	52,801	61,012	62,084	70,295	74,858	8
MO	32,753	32,753	32,753	32,753	32,753	32,753	1
MS	27,488	27,488	27,488	27,488	27,488	27,488	1
MT	49,201	49,771	50,341	50,341	50,910	51,480	3
NJ	47,520	54,150	63,280	61,362	66,570	94,349	8
NM	50,031	50,782	52,073	51,416	52,707	55,430	4
NV	65,000	65,000	65,000	65,000	65,000	65,000	1
NY	56,926	82,648	88,543	92,196	100,518	107,182	6

OH	53,891	59,700	60,956	59,987	64,497	66,706	5
OK	39,028	41,314	43,601	43,601	45,887	48,173	2
OR	50,749	51,080	51,410	51,410	51,741	52,071	2
PA	29,873	38,369	43,741	44,394	48,542	63,181	22
RI	51,831	56,179	57,122	57,860	58,803	60,937	5
SC	45,046	46,285	47,524	47,524	48,762	50,001	3
TN	25,968	29,741	33,514	33,514	37,287	41,060	3
TX	49,705	55,439	60,817	61,173	66,374	71,574	3
VA	60,314	60,368	65,353	64,373	69,358	72,352	4
VT	49,420	55,005	55,472	57,334	57,800	57,800	10
WI	43,912	50,240	53,662	51,313	58,225	63,482	11
WY	41,258	47,914	54,911	59,050	61,944	62,996	6

DEPARTMENT HEAD/COORDINATOR/SENIOR MANAGER—CONTINUED

Large Public Library (serving a population of 100,000 to 499,999)

Regional Data

	Min	Q1	Mean	Median	Q3	Max	N
Great Lakes & Plains	37,065	58,162	77,802	73,026	92,617	153,059	90
North Atlantic	27,745	57,375	76,441	71,199	90,000	167,200	90
Southeast	30,000	59,693	72,572	70,716	80,275	144,115	76
West & Southwest	48,558	71,149	90,413	86,340	109,526	164,559	115
ALL REGIONS	27,745	60,462	80,044	74,722	96,284	167,200	371

State Data

	Min	Q1	Mean	Median	Q3	Max	N
AR	37,479	37,479	37,479	37,479	37,479	37,479	1
AZ	47,242	49,643	58,497	56,431	64,155	79,508	15
CA	54,888	72,268	83,784	81,515	94,530	108,852	40
CO	48,716	59,332	63,867	66,671	69,843	73,494	10
CT	55,850	60,271	62,061	62,246	65,057	68,330	8
FL	39,499	46,587	53,919	52,393	58,935	82,640	54
GA	39,061	44,758	50,436	50,455	56,123	61,791	7
IA	57,560	61,835	69,522	67,415	75,102	85,696	8
IN	43,000	51,719	59,988	60,942	66,467	80,547	43
KS	43,000	51,500	63,659	64,216	73,276	83,075	8
KY	40,600	48,684	54,873	51,456	62,033	70,048	11
LA	41,520	47,790	55,567	57,310	62,890	73,110	40
MA	49,485	54,034	58,583	58,583	63,132	67,681	7
MD	51,551	59,849	68,205	69,262	76,615	86,971	21
MI	50,083	53,946	59,505	57,637	63,568	77,286	27
MO	34,283	47,983	56,758	57,066	62,467	89,116	22
MS	35,704	38,662	49,441	41,620	56,310	71,000	3
NC	37,025	42,572	52,327	49,193	61,934	81,752	39
NE	54,999	57,341	62,119	62,231	65,236	73,588	17

NJ	48,437	57,849	71,668	75,145	83,270	94,474	26
NV	68,931	69,940	70,949	70,949	71,957	72,966	6
NY	66,807	66,807	66,807	66,807	66,807	66,807	10
OH	36,691	51,035	67,262	63,675	78,543	153,059	117
OR	66,243	68,215	70,187	70,187	72,159	74,131	3
PA	35,490	45,649	53,541	53,310	59,065	71,926	38
SC	38,291	44,254	47,101	45,845	51,526	54,569	25
SD	87,526	87,526	87,526	87,526	87,526	87,526	2
TX	38,670	52,558	55,331	55,966	60,659	67,902	41
UT	44,000	44,000	44,000	44,000	44,000	44,000	2
VA	33,813	49,246	53,359	52,932	57,806	74,003	17
WA	67,068	67,068	67,068	67,068	67,068	67,068	3
WI	55,120	55,120	55,120	55,120	55,120	55,120	4

DEPARTMENT HEAD/COORDINATOR/SENIOR MANAGER—CONTINUED

Very Large Public Library (serving a population of 500,000 or more)

Regional Data

	Min	Q1	Mean	Median	Q3	Max	N
Great Lakes & Plains	76,535	82,981	89,919	86,380	110,381	110,381	213
North Atlantic	64,277	80,373	95,457	101,786	115,901	115,901	484
Southeast	73,961	75,720	88,587	84,075	112,237	112,237	350
West & Southwest	70,304	79,710	95,740	94,454	121,493	121,493	504
ALL REGIONS	64,277	77,280	93,422	89,039	121,493	121,493	1,551

State Data

	Min	Q1	Mean	Median	Q3	Max	N
AZ	47,259	57,540	66,045	64,166	71,963	111,758	39
CA	51,238	75,447	82,872	81,272	89,127	120,286	139
CO	47,967	60,431	65,757	66,663	71,143	89,039	34
DC	76,996	80,750	88,468	85,445	91,668	114,950	31
FL	41,040	48,684	59,943	55,530	67,619	112,237	211
GA	45,660	59,519	62,288	64,936	68,064	73,961	74
HI	45,036	50,202	59,781	58,164	69,171	78,024	41
MA	46,274	59,726	66,584	62,731	69,293	101,786	87
MD	42,748	63,032	76,297	76,298	87,222	115,901	101
MN	48,192	62,290	68,384	69,119	77,326	87,630	67
MO	47,967	53,371	59,310	56,442	67,086	76,535	29
NC	46,774	59,533	68,519	67,441	77,146	91,843	31
NJ	54,810	61,687	68,007	68,952	73,788	80,373	29
NV	54,392	65,525	78,572	75,910	87,953	121,493	43
NY	52,278	53,181	57,203	56,487	59,793	64,277	236
OH	44,533	59,866	70,274	70,345	79,900	110,381	101
OK	46,488	63,341	69,758	72,530	76,789	84,768	30
OR	70,681	73,036	82,448	81,888	89,315	99,868	10

TN	35,263	49,828	55,468	54,010	60,195	76,306	34
TX	39,062	49,171	57,756	59,092	66,726	70,304	46
UT	47,712	55,470	61,281	60,564	66,870	74,496	23
WA	61,352	80,050	87,390	87,652	95,254	107,363	99
WI	53,519	60,809	66,963	66,287	74,912	85,129	16

DEPARTMENT HEAD/COORDINATOR/SENIOR MANAGER—CONTINUED
ALL PUBLIC LIBRARIES

Regional Data

	Min	Q1	Mean	Median	Q3	Max	N
Great Lakes & Plains	31,200	53,500	64,010	62,977	72,364	153,059	544
North Atlantic	24,114	53,685	65,492	62,946	76,675	115,901	738
Southeast	25,968	48,017	57,597	55,016	65,633	112,237	568
West & Southwest	38,670	56,114	68,574	66,726	78,287	121,493	671
ALL REGIONS	24,114	52,076	63,531	61,808	72,364	153,059	2,521

State Data

	Min	Q1	Mean	Median	Q3	Max	N
AL	54,905	54,905	54,905	54,905	54,905	54,905	3
AR	37,479	38,545	39,612	39,612	40,678	41,744	2
AZ	47,242	54,513	64,076	63,159	71,238	111,758	54
CA	51,238	74,968	82,947	81,409	90,561	120,286	201
CO	47,967	57,498	64,677	66,400	71,142	89,039	48
CT	55,850	61,724	64,198	63,959	67,659	71,995	28
DC	76,996	80,750	88,468	85,445	91,668	114,950	31
FL	36,000	48,045	58,430	54,481	65,884	112,237	269
GA	39,061	57,353	61,604	64,017	67,982	73,961	81
HI	45,036	50,202	59,781	58,164	69,171	78,024	41
IA	57,560	63,260	69,520	69,514	71,570	85,696	10
IL	33,495	53,297	64,053	62,723	72,503	98,718	37
IN	31,200	50,182	57,193	56,389	64,846	80,547	58
KS	43,000	51,500	63,659	64,216	73,276	83,075	8
KY	40,600	48,684	54,873	51,456	62,033	70,048	11
LA	41,520	47,039	55,080	55,300	62,230	73,110	42
MA	24,114	49,485	57,782	58,747	66,004	101,786	123
MD	42,748	60,756	74,415	74,330	83,508	115,901	122
ME	38,452	40,924	42,968	40,924	47,270	47,270	15
MI	45,020	53,946	59,792	57,637	68,493	77,286	35
MN	48,192	62,290	68,384	69,119	77,326	87,630	67
MO	32,753	50,725	57,512	55,721	65,800	89,116	52
MS	27,488	33,650	43,953	38,662	48,965	71,000	4
MT	49,201	49,771	50,341	50,341	50,910	51,480	3
NC	37,025	48,833	60,295	61,663	69,576	91,843	70
NE	54,999	57,341	62,119	62,231	65,236	73,588	17

NH	37,856	38,272	38,688	38,688	39,104	39,520	3
NJ	28,344	58,000	66,814	66,765	75,545	94,474	73
NM	50,031	50,782	52,073	51,416	52,707	55,430	4
NV	54,392	65,583	77,055	72,966	85,405	121,493	50
NY	52,278	56,816	69,535	61,632	82,152	107,182	264
OH	36,691	56,203	68,479	65,957	78,709	153,059	225
OK	39,028	61,224	67,666	69,684	76,056	84,768	32
OR	50,749	68,462	74,576	73,060	85,259	99,868	15
PA	29,873	43,513	48,593	47,528	53,457	71,926	63
RI	51,831	56,179	57,122	57,860	58,803	60,937	5
SC	38,291	44,393	47,148	45,845	50,999	54,569	28
SD	87,526	87,526	87,526	87,526	87,526	87,526	2
TN	25,968	47,600	54,005	52,988	59,457	76,306	37
TX	38,670	51,233	56,690	56,230	63,107	71,574	90
UT	44,000	54,744	60,530	59,496	66,636	74,496	25
VA	33,813	50,279	55,757	54,152	62,185	74,003	21
VT	49,420	55,005	55,472	57,334	57,800	57,800	10
WA	61,352	78,925	86,713	87,058	94,885	107,363	102
WI	38,948	52,968	61,229	60,643	68,876	85,129	31
WY	41,258	47,914	54,911	59,050	61,944	62,996	6

MANAGER/SUPERVISOR OF SUPPORT STAFF

Persons who supervise support staff in any part of the library but do not supervise professional librarians.
Very Small Public Library (serving a population of less than 10,000)

Regional Data

	Min	Q1	Mean	Median	Q3	Max	N
Great Lakes & Plains	33,807	33,871	40,954	33,935	55,120	55,120	5
North Atlantic	23,036	23,036	23,036	23,036	23,036	23,036	1
ALL REGIONS	23,036	31,114	36,475	33,871	55,120	55,120	6

State Data

	Min	Q1	Mean	Median	Q3	Max	N
IA	30,713	31,519	32,324	32,324	33,130	33,935	2
IL	51,894	52,701	53,507	53,507	54,314	55,120	2
ME	23,036	23,036	23,036	23,036	23,036	23,036	1
OH	33,807	33,807	33,807	33,807	33,807	33,807	1

MANAGER/SUPERVISOR OF SUPPORT STAFF—CONTINUED

Small Public Library (serving a population of 10,000 to 24,999)

Regional Data

	Min	Q1	Mean	Median	Q3	Max	N
Great Lakes & Plains	46,459	47,435	48,411	48,411	50,362	50,362	8
North Atlantic	39,699	44,059	54,655	55,411	69,624	69,624	15

	Min	Q1	Mean	Median	Q3	Max	N
West & Southwest	39,224	41,681	55,793	51,931	80,086	80,086	9
ALL REGIONS	39,224	42,076	53,993	52,092	80,086	80,086	32

State Data

	Min	Q1	Mean	Median	Q3	Max	N
CA	72,847	73,638	75,839	75,212	77,413	80,086	5
CT	53,821	53,821	53,821	53,821	53,821	53,821	1
IL	36,442	40,042	42,101	41,840	45,395	46,459	6
MA	45,318	46,533	51,972	47,140	53,890	66,979	5
ME	37,122	37,766	38,411	38,411	39,055	39,699	2
NJ	57,000	57,000	57,000	57,000	57,000	57,000	1
NY	45,954	50,477	56,859	55,000	62,312	69,624	3
OH	45,324	46,584	47,843	47,843	49,103	50,362	2
PA	36,885	37,865	38,845	38,845	39,825	40,805	2
TX	42,500	42,500	42,500	42,500	42,500	42,500	1
WA	61,362	61,362	61,362	61,362	61,362	61,362	1
WY	35,306	36,286	37,265	37,265	38,245	39,224	2

MANAGER/SUPERVISOR OF SUPPORT STAFF—CONTINUED

Medium Public Library (serving a population of 25,000 to 99,999)

Regional Data

	Min	Q1	Mean	Median	Q3	Max	N
Great Lakes & Plains	43,750	50,669	57,764	57,480	73,086	73,086	39
North Atlantic	40,430	42,580	60,915	65,798	90,898	90,898	33
Southeast	37,020	40,124	49,366	49,564	61,315	61,315	11
West & Southwest	40,815	44,300	53,577	46,393	84,300	84,300	31
ALL REGIONS	37,020	43,871	55,871	49,494	90,898	90,898	114

State Data

	Min	Q1	Mean	Median	Q3	Max	N
AL	41,158	41,158	41,158	41,158	41,158	41,158	1
AR	57,969	57,969	57,969	57,969	57,969	57,969	1
CA	46,342	64,668	67,754	71,286	73,791	80,520	10
CO	44,096	45,289	46,481	46,481	47,674	48,866	4
CT	51,698	58,450	63,242	65,201	69,015	72,828	3
IA	51,901	55,093	58,284	58,284	61,476	64,667	2
ID	37,200	38,975	40,750	40,750	42,525	44,300	2
IL	39,199	54,391	58,850	61,534	66,038	73,086	10
IN	27,300	30,757	39,492	43,045	44,050	52,310	12
MA	44,235	44,235	44,235	44,235	44,235	44,235	4
ME	35,694	35,694	38,309	38,309	40,924	40,924	8
MO	38,500	39,813	41,125	41,125	42,438	43,750	2
MT	48,284	48,289	48,293	48,293	48,298	48,302	2
NJ	58,710	60,482	62,254	62,254	64,026	65,798	2

NM	46,393	46,393	46,393	46,393	46,393	46,393	1
NV	45,000	45,000	45,000	45,000	45,000	45,000	2
NY	64,406	72,882	78,887	81,358	86,128	90,898	3
OH	30,900	40,030	49,471	51,480	59,997	62,649	10
OR	43,695	43,695	43,695	43,695	43,695	43,695	1
PA	26,000	32,963	35,513	36,000	40,118	40,430	8
RI	48,727	50,278	57,283	51,829	61,561	71,292	5
SC	31,849	33,996	35,004	36,142	36,581	37,020	3
TX	35,557	37,424	38,778	39,369	40,723	40,815	6
VA	28,093	37,064	45,147	46,034	53,675	61,315	6
WI	45,406	47,356	48,278	49,306	49,714	50,122	3
WY	59,120	70,160	74,873	81,200	82,750	84,300	3

MANAGER/SUPERVISOR OF SUPPORT STAFF—CONTINUED

Large Public Library (serving a population of 100,000 to 499,999)

Regional Data

	Min	Q1	Mean	Median	Q3	Max	N
Great Lakes & Plains	55,120	63,392	66,818	67,488	76,981	76,981	109
North Atlantic	42,488	53,478	59,145	57,940	75,674	75,674	72
Southeast	45,136	52,518	57,461	57,746	69,460	69,460	125
West & Southwest	53,976	62,230	69,590	68,035	91,968	91,968	90
ALL REGIONS	42,488	56,745	63,527	63,504	91,968	91,968	396

State Data

	Min	Q1	Mean	Median	Q3	Max	N
AZ	45,643	47,239	56,694	56,286	65,741	68,562	1
CA	51,204	64,526	72,496	74,542	78,824	91,968	43
CO	55,511	58,725	61,939	61,939	65,152	68,366	3
CT	68,395	68,395	68,395	68,395	68,395	68,395	1
FL	33,141	42,348	48,350	46,853	52,046	69,460	35
GA	32,198	44,572	50,392	52,544	57,985	62,889	7
ID	53,976	53,976	53,976	53,976	53,976	53,976	3
IN	36,795	42,206	47,770	44,762	51,356	69,868	38
KS	41,600	50,397	58,853	61,381	67,842	72,030	8
KY	39,956	41,251	42,546	42,546	43,841	45,136	2
LA	42,973	52,658	51,519	53,040	54,163	54,759	7
MA	37,275	37,937	42,202	39,548	43,813	52,436	18
MD	41,968	47,179	49,983	48,174	53,075	59,274	15
MI	56,359	57,760	62,335	61,438	66,013	70,106	5
MO	46,710	56,103	56,478	56,591	58,870	64,118	5
MS	25,000	38,379	43,434	46,000	50,000	57,165	21
NC	33,753	37,996	39,608	40,263	41,582	45,795	19
NE	47,571	48,705	52,571	51,496	54,541	65,107	22
NJ	48,437	63,690	64,155	64,312	67,499	75,674	22

NV	51,711	54,371	57,596	57,075	57,117	67,704	5
NY	49,246	51,086	52,926	52,926	54,765	56,605	11
OH	24,876	38,741	41,971	43,669	45,259	61,214	19
OR	58,213	61,968	67,557	66,505	70,633	82,979	9
PA	37,011	40,163	40,538	41,326	41,700	42,488	5
SC	32,000	39,568	41,747	41,312	42,803	58,327	14
SD	61,818	64,345	68,900	68,318	72,998	76,981	11
TX	29,657	41,050	44,654	44,495	49,966	60,281	20
VA	36,915	43,481	47,669	47,267	51,055	66,160	20
WA	62,880	62,880	62,880	62,880	62,880	62,880	2
WI	55,120	55,120	55,120	55,120	55,120	55,120	1

MANAGER/SUPERVISOR OF SUPPORT STAFF—CONTINUED

Very Large Public Library (serving a population of 500,000 or more)

Regional Data

	Min	Q1	Mean	Median	Q3	Max	N
Great Lakes & Plains	62,694	67,848	72,296	73,002	81,192	81,192	102
North Atlantic	56,638	70,634	76,470	77,650	93,944	93,944	105
Southeast	51,311	52,031	65,621	64,886	81,402	81,402	183
West & Southwest	41,938	69,807	75,916	77,989	97,647	97,647	182
ALL REGIONS	41,938	64,701	73,294	75,299	97,647	97,647	572

State Data

	Min	Q1	Mean	Median	Q3	Max	N
AZ	49,150	50,981	57,671	53,373	60,345	81,494	29
CA	53,858	61,090	68,845	74,256	76,788	81,868	30
CO	40,934	54,134	57,236	57,661	62,438	70,840	13
DC	76,996	77,747	78,498	78,498	79,249	80,000	2
FL	38,130	48,786	55,054	53,955	61,342	81,402	94
GA	38,316	46,275	52,768	52,308	57,843	77,501	68
HI	43,296	50,688	56,265	57,024	61,680	66,708	18
MA	42,000	45,659	49,319	49,322	52,980	56,638	35
MD	40,275	48,854	60,744	61,084	69,864	93,944	52
MO	42,778	47,656	53,718	51,940	57,866	73,002	46
NC	50,080	51,489	51,625	52,075	52,211	52,271	4
NJ	48,836	49,147	54,130	49,609	53,205	75,299	16
NV	46,488	55,463	65,840	63,606	72,977	92,352	34
OH	40,456	51,674	58,475	58,365	64,035	81,192	55
OK	41,628	51,323	58,371	58,110	64,781	74,484	27
TN	44,077	46,805	47,789	47,541	49,163	51,311	17
TX	41,938	41,938	41,938	41,938	41,938	41,938	27
WA	89,513	90,394	92,812	91,275	94,461	97,647	4
WI	62,694	62,694	62,694	62,694	62,694	62,694	1

Regional Data

	Min	Q1	Mean	Median	Q3	Max	N
Great Lakes & Plains	24,876	45,007	52,671	51,428	60,744	81,192	263
North Atlantic	23,036	45,160	55,054	52,842	64,733	93,944	224
Southeast	25,000	42,086	48,848	48,217	54,621	81,402	319
West & Southwest	29,657	49,988	59,903	58,045	69,807	97,647	309
ALL REGIONS	23,036	45,038	53,877	51,895	62,243	97,647	1,115

State Data

	Min	Q1	Mean	Median	Q3	Max	N
AL	41,158	41,158	41,158	41,158	41,158	41,158	1
AR	57,969	57,969	57,969	57,969	57,969	57,969	1
AZ	45,643	50,487	57,501	53,373	63,146	81,494	33
CA	46,342	62,862	71,235	74,001	77,666	91,968	88
CO	40,934	49,937	56,479	56,662	62,438	70,840	20
CT	51,698	53,821	62,389	65,201	68,395	72,828	5
DC	76,996	76,996	76,996	76,996	76,996	76,996	1
FL	33,141	45,591	52,252	51,088	56,909	81,402	129
GA	32,198	45,921	52,330	52,426	57,850	77,501	75
HI	43,296	50,688	56,265	57,024	61,680	66,708	18
IA	30,713	33,130	45,304	42,918	55,093	64,667	4
ID	37,200	40,750	45,159	44,300	49,138	53,976	5
IL	36,442	43,685	52,673	53,055	61,952	73,086	18
IN	27,300	41,808	46,761	44,548	51,355	69,868	50
KS	41,600	50,397	58,853	61,381	67,842	72,030	8
KY	39,956	41,251	42,546	42,546	43,841	45,136	2
LA	42,973	52,658	51,519	53,040	54,163	54,759	7
MA	37,275	44,235	48,126	46,878	52,436	66,979	62
MD	40,275	47,179	57,635	53,078	64,401	93,944	67
ME	23,036	35,694	36,156	37,122	40,312	40,924	11
MI	56,359	57,760	62,335	61,438	66,013	70,106	5
MO	38,500	47,386	53,481	51,972	57,915	73,002	53
MS	25,000	38,379	43,434	46,000	50,000	57,165	21
MT	48,284	48,289	48,293	48,293	48,298	48,302	0
NC	33,753	38,976	43,041	41,493	49,009	52,271	23
NE	47,571	48,705	52,571	51,496	54,541	65,107	22
NJ	48,437	53,244	60,884	63,924	65,670	75,674	41
NM	46,393	46,393	46,393	46,393	46,393	46,393	1
NV	45,000	54,371	62,885	58,781	68,827	92,352	41
NY	45,954	53,562	64,136	60,506	72,558	90,898	17
OH	24,876	45,046	52,935	53,144	61,328	81,192	87
OK	41,628	51,323	58,371	58,110	64,781	74,484	27

2012 ALA-APA Salary Survey: Librarian—Public and Academic

Public (Very Small to Very Large; Regional, State)

OR	43,695	60,861	64,574	64,349	70,153	82,979	10
PA	26,000	36,000	37,572	39,936	40,805	42,488	15
RI	48,727	50,278	57,283	51,829	61,561	71,292	4
SC	31,849	37,020	40,557	40,244	42,624	58,327	17
SD	61,818	64,345	68,900	68,318	72,998	76,981	11
TN	44,077	46,805	47,789	47,541	49,163	51,311	17
TX	29,657	40,568	43,420	41,938	46,874	60,281	54
VA	28,093	43,444	47,291	47,045	51,065	66,160	26
WA	61,362	62,880	80,535	89,513	91,275	97,647	7
WI	45,406	49,306	52,530	50,122	55,120	62,694	5
WY	35,306	39,224	59,830	59,120	81,200	84,300	5

LIBRARIAN WHO DOES NOT SUPERVISE

Full-time staff with master's degrees from programs in library and information studies accredited by the ALA who were not reported earlier and who do not supervise.

Very Small Public Library (serving a population of less than 10,000)

Regional Data

	Min	Q1	Mean	Median	Q3	Max	N
Great Lakes & Plains	58,267	58,267	58,267	58,267	58,267	58,267	3
North Atlantic	25,708	39,170	41,811	44,442	51,733	51,733	12
ALL REGIONS	25,708	40,488	44,553	46,221	58,267	58,267	15

State Data

	Min	Q1	Mean	Median	Q3	Max	N
CT	48,000	48,000	48,000	48,000	48,000	48,000	1
IL	46,443	48,345	51,652	50,247	54,257	58,267	3
MA	39,170	39,170	39,170	39,170	39,170	39,170	1
ME	22,477	23,296	24,100	24,115	24,912	25,708	3
NJ	50,400	50,733	51,067	51,067	51,400	51,733	3
NY	40,785	41,699	42,614	42,614	43,528	44,442	2

LIBRARIAN WHO DOES NOT SUPERVISE—CONTINUED

Small Public Library (serving a population of 10,000 to 24,999)

Regional Data

	Min	Q1	Mean	Median	Q3	Max	N
Great Lakes & Plains	27,123	38,546	45,473	49,969	59,328	59,328	13
North Atlantic	34,093	42,259	56,151	53,890	99,318	99,318	48
Southeast	34,500	34,500	34,500	34,500	34,500	34,500	1
West & Southwest	45,792	51,837	57,272	57,882	68,143	68,143	7
ALL REGIONS	27,123	41,548	52,557	51,930	99,318	99,318	69

State Data

	Min	Q1	Mean	Median	Q3	Max	N
CA	62,817	64,400	65,647	65,982	67,063	68,143	3
FL	34,500	34,500	34,500	34,500	34,500	34,500	1
IL	39,990	40,612	46,426	44,969	48,846	59,328	7
KS	27,123	27,123	27,123	27,123	27,123	27,123	1
MA	41,144	44,142	47,391	47,140	50,515	53,890	9
ME	23,400	34,205	34,624	35,008	39,668	40,837	6
NJ	24,000	50,484	50,623	55,000	58,630	65,000	7
NY	41,028	49,334	57,214	53,795	60,392	99,318	20
OH	37,128	38,711	42,759	41,969	46,016	49,969	4
PA	33,620	33,738	33,857	33,857	33,975	34,093	2
RI	43,680	43,680	43,680	43,680	43,680	43,680	2
TX	45,495	48,592	51,689	51,689	54,785	57,882	2
VT	56,238	56,238	56,238	56,238	56,238	56,238	1
WY	41,096	42,270	43,444	43,444	44,618	45,792	2

LIBRARIAN WHO DOES NOT SUPERVISE—CONTINUED

Medium Public Library (serving a population of 25,000 to 99,999)

Regional Data

	Min	Q1	Mean	Median	Q3	Max	N
Great Lakes & Plains	22,658	41,865	49,517	49,465	57,612	77,661	119
North Atlantic	25,899	40,317	52,378	52,569	60,933	100,260	102
Southeast	26,749	39,255	41,413	41,299	44,104	53,321	42
West & Southwest	28,704	40,809	48,431	45,355	55,286	76,505	49
ALL REGIONS	22,658	40,608	49,210	49,000	56,491	100,260	312

State Data

	Min	Q1	Mean	Median	Q3	Max	N
AL	37,564	37,564	37,564	37,564	37,564	37,564	15
AR	34,086	38,970	40,935	39,540	41,329	50,751	6
CA	45,552	58,665	63,551	64,331	71,319	76,505	21
CO	33,912	39,974	42,852	43,576	46,454	50,345	4
CT	53,016	55,935	56,544	56,531	57,914	58,565	15
IA	33,579	47,759	52,083	55,723	60,958	62,462	13
IL	22,658	45,584	51,569	51,227	58,622	77,661	45
IN	24,414	26,884	31,200	33,317	34,462	35,651	29
KY	28,558	28,558	28,558	28,558	28,558	28,558	1
LA	26,749	31,148	35,547	35,547	39,946	44,345	2
MA	25,899	35,053	39,757	43,549	44,715	49,991	22
ME	32,176	32,176	34,692	34,692	37,208	37,208	4
MI	39,200	49,475	59,436	58,370	72,838	73,858	10
MO	37,803	37,803	37,803	37,803	37,803	37,803	1
MT	28,704	33,600	34,351	33,696	36,712	39,041	4

NJ	45,800	50,383	53,491	52,530	54,498	66,344	10
NM	40,354	40,657	47,585	40,960	51,201	61,441	7
NY	49,711	55,537	65,760	65,901	71,243	100,260	30
OH	37,190	46,248	48,910	49,465	51,542	58,156	15
PA	26,000	33,717	36,105	34,762	38,450	49,815	16
RI	46,769	46,853	49,656	46,937	51,100	55,263	7
SC	40,582	41,192	41,802	41,802	42,412	43,022	2
TN	35,038	35,564	40,360	36,089	43,022	49,954	3
TX	31,170	41,684	46,289	46,673	50,347	57,715	13
VA	40,180	41,051	43,966	43,093	44,343	53,321	13
WI	40,000	44,351	46,134	47,029	48,812	50,480	6

LIBRARIAN WHO DOES NOT SUPERVISE—CONTINUED

Large Public Library (serving a population of 100,000 to 499,999)

Regional Data

	Min	Q1	Mean	Median	Q3	Max	N
Great Lakes & Plains	46,904	58,838	65,863	64,495	96,034	96,034	205
North Atlantic	45,254	50,856	59,279	61,422	70,117	70,117	122
Southeast	48,000	55,960	59,536	61,945	66,732	66,732	173
West & Southwest	43,031	47,767	54,955	52,493	76,404	76,404	402
ALL REGIONS	43,031	50,552	59,973	61,422	96,034	96,034	902

State Data

	Min	Q1	Mean	Median	Q3	Max	N
AZ	39,542	43,996	52,492	52,927	57,426	69,452	22
CA	42,144	57,960	62,918	63,204	67,163	96,034	80
CO	28,476	51,487	52,165	53,760	56,659	64,168	18
CT	53,588	54,322	55,055	55,055	55,789	56,522	10
FL	22,335	38,405	41,607	41,216	44,624	59,610	46
GA	38,000	58,666	60,184	66,673	68,191	69,390	9
IA	50,717	53,922	57,591	57,054	61,442	64,821	11
ID	46,904	46,904	46,904	46,904	46,904	46,904	1
IN	23,962	37,981	44,288	44,107	50,134	70,117	56
KS	33,000	43,583	48,626	48,577	54,048	61,422	29
KY	31,000	36,857	38,682	37,960	39,852	50,856	10
LA	23,125	44,416	41,141	44,637	44,797	45,254	8
MD	41,379	43,395	49,552	44,316	53,500	68,747	18
MI	41,642	44,887	49,887	49,734	53,032	62,372	36
MO	31,179	42,087	48,405	49,471	54,317	64,118	16
MS	29,073	35,768	39,268	40,000	43,500	48,000	4
NC	33,753	37,803	43,645	40,582	49,074	61,517	36
NE	44,466	52,366	57,814	58,096	64,476	66,732	13
NJ	41,842	47,814	52,457	53,740	56,426	66,108	49
NV	53,040	54,330	55,619	55,619	56,909	58,198	2

NY	49,246	49,246	49,246	49,246	49,246	49,246	16
OH	31,595	35,734	46,624	41,600	56,878	76,404	191
OR	42,761	47,069	54,200	54,433	62,192	66,221	26
PA	39,146	41,964	45,645	44,019	48,551	55,473	59
SC	32,000	37,305	40,839	41,285	44,610	50,552	29
TX	22,890	41,985	45,661	45,648	49,076	66,726	77
UT	44,000	44,000	44,000	44,000	44,000	44,000	1
VA	29,835	37,105	38,349	40,816	40,958	43,031	6
WI	44,343	45,513	46,683	46,683	47,853	49,023	10

LIBRARIAN WHO DOES NOT SUPERVISE—CONTINUED

Very Large Public Library (serving a population of 500,000 or more)

Regional Data

	Min	Q1	Mean	Median	Q3	Max	N
Great Lakes & Plains	57,139	59,105	64,549	65,115	70,826	70,826	300
North Atlantic	49,789	68,350	72,937	68,786	89,596	89,596	608
Southeast	50,743	61,058	64,962	67,790	73,524	73,524	387
West & Southwest	57,345	63,218	74,058	71,322	104,045	104,045	728
ALL REGIONS	49,789	62,301	70,579	70,470	104,045	104,045	2,023

State Data

	Min	Q1	Mean	Median	Q3	Max	N
AZ	40,331	45,414	52,941	50,380	61,041	76,946	87
CA	51,238	63,161	69,446	68,325	74,393	96,470	120
CO	38,085	44,949	51,567	49,733	59,835	71,292	48
DC	54,633	60,340	68,673	66,047	77,750	88,166	70
FL	35,661	40,027	46,922	46,216	50,612	71,084	204
GA	36,492	45,684	52,169	52,966	59,265	73,524	90
HI	41,628	45,948	51,074	50,688	55,926	61,680	68
MA	56,638	56,934	60,364	57,042	62,419	68,786	7
MD	34,810	43,589	57,400	55,946	67,857	89,596	100
MN	40,248	47,154	51,224	51,917	54,916	59,760	80
MO	41,085	44,061	48,799	46,568	52,315	70,826	25
NC	37,440	49,612	52,151	51,942	55,114	64,496	54
NJ	44,000	52,075	56,285	55,058	61,200	68,350	55
NV	49,488	54,392	59,944	58,781	63,606	74,422	18
NY	42,638	43,578	46,274	46,396	48,941	49,789	376
OH	40,456	47,406	53,859	53,144	58,490	70,470	148
OK	37,332	45,942	51,135	50,565	55,257	71,352	73
OR	51,128	53,916	56,882	56,765	59,761	62,922	62
TN	32,956	39,097	41,822	41,903	44,821	50,743	39
TX	40,102	42,921	48,983	51,282	52,264	57,345	40

UT	39,720	47,280	51,884	50,232	56,052	64,104	45
WA	51,376	61,541	70,598	70,314	78,661	104,045	167
WI	39,952	49,355	50,747	51,637	53,733	57,139	47

LIBRARIAN WHO DOES NOT SUPERVISE—CONTINUED
ALL PUBLIC LIBRARIES

Regional Data

	Min	Q1	Mean	Median	Q3	Max	N
Great Lakes & Plains	22,658	41,969	48,889	48,665	54,794	77,661	797
North Atlantic	22,477	43,967	53,376	53,016	59,874	100,260	920
Southeast	22,335	39,509	45,659	43,985	50,669	73,524	578
West & Southwest	22,890	45,482	53,551	51,888	61,122	104,045	1,011
ALL REGIONS	22,335	42,462	50,276	49,128	56,894	104,045	3,305

State Data

	Min	Q1	Mean	Median	Q3	Max	N
AL	37,564	37,564	37,564	37,564	37,564	37,564	1
AR	34,086	43,931	51,735	50,055	58,986	76,946	118
CA	42,144	60,144	64,639	64,356	68,325	96,470	79
CO	28,476	45,157	51,067	51,000	57,336	71,292	58
CT	48,000	54,054	55,392	56,471	57,362	58,565	11
DC	54,633	60,340	68,673	66,047	77,750	88,166	14
FL	22,335	39,180	45,383	43,331	49,078	71,084	289
GA	36,492	45,684	53,036	53,623	59,677	73,524	60
HI	41,628	45,948	51,074	50,688	55,926	61,680	28
IA	33,579	52,358	54,202	57,054	61,442	64,821	32
ID	46,904	46,904	46,904	46,904	46,904	46,904	1
IL	22,658	44,558	50,991	50,000	58,267	77,661	94
IN	23,962	35,979	42,543	42,746	49,283	70,117	69
KS	27,123	43,555	47,885	48,513	53,920	61,422	62
KY	28,558	35,407	37,669	37,409	39,467	50,856	20
LA	23,125	39,946	39,742	44,469	44,732	45,254	20
MA	25,899	39,664	46,721	45,023	55,951	68,786	18
MD	34,810	43,589	55,631	52,938	65,272	89,596	109
ME	22,477	28,146	32,589	34,205	37,208	40,837	13
MI	39,200	46,088	52,458	50,252	57,293	73,858	35
MN	40,248	47,154	51,224	51,917	54,916	59,760	11
MO	31,179	43,739	48,387	47,181	53,626	70,826	51
MS	29,073	35,768	39,268	40,000	43,500	48,000	4
MT	28,704	33,600	34,351	33,696	36,712	39,041	6
NC	33,753	42,767	49,316	50,413	54,802	64,496	83
NE	25,708	51,714	54,603	56,586	63,984	66,732	55
NJ	24,000	49,299	53,968	53,811	59,243	68,350	266
NM	40,354	40,657	47,585	40,960	51,201	61,441	4

	Min	Q1	Mean	Median	Q3	Max	N
NV	49,488	53,716	59,157	58,198	62,390	74,422	16
NY	40,785	49,789	59,306	54,807	66,567	100,260	116
OH	31,595	40,030	49,402	48,534	57,023	76,404	317
OK	37,332	45,942	51,135	50,565	55,257	71,352	119
OR	42,761	49,524	55,059	55,933	61,134	66,221	32
PA	26,000	36,291	41,865	41,767	46,767	55,473	56
RI	43,680	45,997	48,162	46,853	49,019	55,263	4
SC	32,000	37,488	40,903	41,479	44,547	50,552	420
TN	32,956	38,566	41,791	41,903	44,948	50,743	74
TX	41,257	43,887	45,584	45,074	47,169	50,743	15
UT	39,720	46,452	51,555	49,872	55,458	64,104	42
VA	29,835	40,680	42,406	41,572	43,706	53,321	73
VT	56,238	56,238	56,238	56,238	56,238	56,238	1
WA	51,376	61,541	70,598	70,314	78,661	104,045	137
WI	39,952	45,653	49,086	49,497	52,509	57,139	34
WY	41,096	42,270	43,444	43,444	44,618	45,792	2

BEGINNING LIBRARIAN

Full-time staff hired in the last six months with master's degrees from programs in library and information studies accredited by the ALA, but with no professional experience after receiving the degree.

Very Small Public Library (serving a population of less than 10,000)

Regional Data

	Min	Q1	Mean	Median	Q3	Max	N
North Atlantic	24,115	26,959	29,803	29,803	32,646	35,490	3
ALL REGIONS	24,115	26,959	29,803	29,803	32,646	35,490	3

State Data

	Min	Q1	Mean	Median	Q3	Max	N
MA	35,490	35,490	35,490	35,490	35,490	35,490	1
ME	24,115	24,115	24,115	24,115	24,115	24,115	1

BEGINNING LIBRARIAN—CONTINUED

Small Public Library (serving a population of 10,000 to 24,999)

Regional Data

	Min	Q1	Mean	Median	Q3	Max	N
Great Lakes & Plains	39,990	40,188	40,385	40,385	40,780	40,780	5
North Atlantic	44,000	45,882	47,763	47,763	51,526	51,526	5
Southeast	30,000	30,000	30,000	30,000	30,000	30,000	1
ALL REGIONS	30,000	39,990	41,259	40,780	51,526	51,526	11

State Data

	Min	Q1	Mean	Median	Q3	Max	N
FL	30,000	30,000	30,000	30,000	30,000	30,000	1
IL	31,000	34,500	36,330	38,000	38,995	39,990	4
NJ	42,000	42,871	45,756	43,741	47,634	51,526	3
NY	35,000	37,250	39,500	39,500	41,750	44,000	2
WI	40,780	40,780	40,780	40,780	40,780	40,780	1

BEGINNING LIBRARIAN—CONTINUED

Medium Public Library (serving a population of 25,000 to 99,999)

Regional Data

	Min	Q1	Mean	Median	Q3	Max	N
Great Lakes & Plains	26,972	39,915	44,907	47,777	59,946	59,946	22
North Atlantic	35,000	37,208	45,314	45,800	56,986	56,986	8
Southeast	29,868	31,513	34,749	34,341	40,997	40,997	9
West & Southwest	32,500	34,375	38,319	37,455	45,867	45,867	8
ALL REGIONS	26,972	34,671	40,954	39,910	59,946	59,946	47

State Data

	Min	Q1	Mean	Median	Q3	Max	N
IA	49,926	49,926	49,926	49,926	49,926	49,926	1
IL	36,483	37,010	37,978	37,537	38,726	39,915	7
MO	26,972	26,972	26,972	26,972	26,972	26,972	1
OH	43,264	44,392	45,521	45,521	46,649	47,777	4
WI	45,631	48,302	51,230	49,671	52,598	59,946	9
CT	51,578	51,578	51,578	51,578	51,578	51,578	1
ME	37,208	37,208	37,208	37,208	37,208	37,208	2
NJ	45,800	45,800	45,800	45,800	45,800	45,800	1
NY	56,986	56,986	56,986	56,986	56,986	56,986	1
PA	30,551	31,276	32,517	32,000	33,500	35,000	3
AL	31,513	31,513	31,513	31,513	31,513	31,513	4
LA	37,544	38,407	39,271	39,271	40,134	40,997	2
SC	29,868	29,868	29,868	29,868	29,868	29,868	1
TN	34,341	34,341	34,341	34,341	34,341	34,341	1
VA	37,028	37,028	37,028	37,028	37,028	37,028	1
CA	45,867	45,867	45,867	45,867	45,867	45,867	1
ID	35,000	35,000	35,000	35,000	35,000	35,000	2
TX	39,910	39,910	39,910	39,910	39,910	39,910	3
WY	32,500	32,500	32,500	32,500	32,500	32,500	2

BEGINNING LIBRARIAN—CONTINUED

Large Public Library (serving a population of 100,000 to 499,999)

Regional Data

	Min	Q1	Mean	Median	Q3	Max	N
Great Lakes & Plains	37,727	41,501	43,507	42,994	50,734	50,734	18
North Atlantic	39,146	40,537	42,221	41,484	46,772	46,772	21
Southeast	25,000	32,538	37,575	34,237	58,960	58,960	63
West & Southwest	47,923	52,732	55,222	57,540	60,203	60,203	44
ALL REGIONS	25,000	37,413	42,931	42,241	60,203	60,203	146

State Data

	Min	Q1	Mean	Median	Q3	Max	N
IA	42,144	50,201	53,331	55,081	57,332	60,203	21
KS	38,117	39,408	40,699	40,699	41,990	43,281	10
MI	31,075	31,075	31,075	31,075	31,075	31,075	1
MO	43,472	43,472	43,472	43,472	43,472	43,472	1
NE	42,515	42,515	42,515	42,515	42,515	42,515	1
OH	34,237	34,237	34,237	34,237	34,237	34,237	6
MA	37,660	40,613	46,170	44,210	49,188	58,960	37
MD	46,772	46,772	46,772	46,772	46,772	46,772	14
NJ	41,967	41,967	41,967	41,967	41,967	41,967	1
PA	50,734	50,734	50,734	50,734	50,734	50,734	1
FL	37,727	37,727	37,727	37,727	37,727	37,727	1
GA	22,000	22,750	23,500	23,500	24,250	25,000	3
KY	33,753	34,433	35,113	35,113	35,792	36,472	4
LA	45,428	45,428	45,428	45,428	45,428	45,428	2
MS	41,000	41,000	41,000	41,000	41,000	41,000	1
NC	34,340	36,173	37,836	38,006	39,585	41,163	12
SC	28,000	33,003	35,051	38,006	38,576	39,146	5
CA	34,000	34,000	34,000	34,000	34,000	34,000	1
TX	32,782	35,837	40,349	42,524	42,679	47,923	11
WA	57,540	57,540	57,540	57,540	57,540	57,540	9

BEGINNING LIBRARIAN—CONTINUED

Very Large Public Library (serving a population of 500,000 or more)

Regional Data

	Min	Q1	Mean	Median	Q3	Max	N
Great Lakes & Plains	43,956	50,430	56,904	56,904	63,378	69,852	75
North Atlantic	36,676	42,169	46,734	46,661	51,226	56,937	24
Southeast	37,351	43,112	48,746	48,873	54,444	60,014	129
West & Southwest	40,020	40,891	49,165	44,290	49,848	74,932	174
ALL REGIONS	36,676	41,451	49,465	46,009	54,033	74,932	402

State Data

	Min	Q1	Mean	Median	Q3	Max	N
OH	27,393	44,087	50,158	51,297	58,553	69,852	74
WI	43,956	43,956	43,956	43,956	43,956	43,956	1
DC	45,345	48,605	51,383	50,417	55,488	56,937	12
MA	46,273	47,620	48,187	48,967	49,145	49,322	4
MD	33,126	34,821	35,439	36,516	36,596	36,676	7
NJ	44,000	44,000	44,000	44,000	44,000	44,000	1
FL	35,531	38,500	41,262	41,471	41,933	48,873	7
GA	52,571	53,746	56,867	58,579	59,368	60,014	116
TN	32,754	34,470	35,431	36,186	36,769	37,351	6
AZ	40,331	40,331	40,331	40,331	40,331	40,331	2
CA	44,117	55,806	61,295	61,646	67,829	74,932	133
CO	42,141	42,249	42,356	42,356	42,464	42,571	2
HI	40,020	40,020	40,020	40,020	40,020	40,020	7
OR	51,128	51,128	51,128	51,128	51,128	51,128	1
TX	34,403	35,089	37,658	35,089	38,126	46,009	29

BEGINNING LIBRARIAN—CONTINUED
ALL PUBLIC LIBRARIES

Regional Data

	Min	Q1	Mean	Median	Q3	Max	N
Great Lakes & Plains	26,972	39,953	46,814	45,873	53,361	69,852	119
North Atlantic	24,115	36,942	42,541	43,741	47,862	56,986	60
Southeast	22,000	37,631	46,162	44,965	56,521	60,014	201
West & Southwest	32,500	39,726	48,320	45,867	57,059	74,932	223
ALL REGIONS	22,000	38,117	46,168	44,770	53,787	74,932	603

State Data

	Min	Q1	Mean	Median	Q3	Max	N
AL	31,513	31,513	31,513	31,513	31,513	31,513	4
AZ	39,542	39,739	39,937	39,937	40,134	40,331	2
CA	42,144	51,850	57,698	57,586	63,850	74,932	155
CO	42,141	42,249	42,356	42,356	42,464	42,571	2
CT	47,481	48,505	49,530	49,530	50,554	51,578	1
DC	45,345	48,605	51,383	50,417	55,488	56,937	12
FL	30,000	37,471	39,713	39,986	42,270	48,873	18
GA	31,075	53,623	55,835	58,579	59,265	60,014	117
HI	40,020	40,020	40,020	40,020	40,020	40,020	7

IA	43,472	45,086	46,699	46,699	48,313	49,926	2
ID	35,000	35,000	35,000	35,000	35,000	35,000	2
IL	31,000	36,747	37,154	37,769	39,436	39,990	11
IN	30,757	30,757	30,757	30,757	30,757	30,757	0
KS	42,515	42,515	42,515	42,515	42,515	42,515	1
KY	34,237	34,237	34,237	34,237	34,237	34,237	6
LA	37,544	40,242	45,497	43,015	48,500	58,960	39
MA	35,490	43,560	44,849	46,273	47,870	49,322	19
MD	33,126	35,669	37,071	36,596	37,999	41,967	8
ME	24,115	30,662	32,844	37,208	37,208	37,208	3
MI	49,734	49,734	49,734	49,734	49,734	49,734	1
MO	26,972	29,661	32,350	32,350	35,038	37,727	2
MS	22,000	22,750	23,500	23,500	24,250	25,000	3
NC	33,753	34,433	35,113	35,113	35,792	36,472	4
NE	42,498	43,231	43,963	43,963	44,696	45,428	2
NJ	41,000	42,435	44,678	43,871	45,350	51,526	6
NY	35,000	39,717	44,045	44,000	44,522	56,986	3
OH	27,393	42,750	49,347	50,133	56,827	69,852	89
OR	51,128	51,128	51,128	51,128	51,128	51,128	1
PA	28,000	30,913	33,784	33,500	37,255	39,146	8
SC	29,868	30,901	31,934	31,934	32,967	34,000	2
TN	32,754	33,944	35,158	35,264	36,478	37,351	7
TX	32,782	34,938	38,808	37,492	42,584	47,923	43
VA	37,028	37,028	37,028	37,028	37,028	37,028	1
WA	57,540	57,540	57,540	57,540	57,540	57,540	9
WI	40,780	44,193	47,726	45,631	49,671	59,946	11
WY	32,500	32,500	32,500	32,500	32,500	32,500	2

Academic (Two-Year College to University; Regional, State)

DIRECTOR/DEAN/CHIEF OFFICER

Chief officer of the library or library system.

Two-Year College

Regional Data

	Min	Q1	Mean	Median	Q3	Max	N
Great Lakes & Plains	43,250	54,809	62,829	65,010	67,854	80,867	11
North Atlantic	57,766	62,299	73,239	70,068	78,035	107,461	8
Southeast	44,600	57,000	63,448	62,733	74,000	80,000	32
West & Southwest	42,000	63,513	75,191	74,895	91,250	101,241	12
ALL REGIONS	42,000	57,771	67,382	65,145	76,024	107,461	63

State Data

	Min	Q1	Mean	Median	Q3	Max	N
AL	51,017	59,843	65,248	68,669	72,364	76,059	3
GA	57,000	61,500	66,000	66,000	70,500	75,000	2
IA	65,280	69,100	72,920	72,920	76,740	80,560	2
IN	52,000	56,250	60,500	60,500	64,750	69,000	2
KS	43,250	47,143	51,037	51,037	54,930	58,823	2
LA	45,000	52,100	61,400	59,200	69,600	80,000	12
MD	59,160	61,586	66,740	64,011	70,530	77,049	3
MO	54,346	54,809	58,775	55,271	60,990	66,708	3
NC	44,600	54,074	59,154	59,028	61,068	77,000	5
NY	57,766	60,556	67,368	63,345	72,169	80,992	3
SC	53,667	57,000	66,917	73,000	75,000	75,919	5
TN	59,700	61,850	62,567	64,000	64,000	64,000	3
TX	42,000	47,343	60,228	61,741	74,626	75,432	4
UT	57,784	67,362	76,940	76,940	86,518	96,096	2
WA	65,422	74,631	80,421	83,840	87,920	92,000	3

DIRECTOR/DEAN/CHIEF OFFICER—CONTINUED

Four-Year College

Regional Data

	Min	Q1	Mean	Median	Q3	Max	N
Great Lakes & Plains	47,800	54,396	69,913	69,000	84,811	100,000	21
North Atlantic	56,654	65,922	94,246	83,929	126,166	166,700	20
Southeast	32,000	51,664	65,665	60,000	76,316	125,000	29
West & Southwest	50,309	58,420	83,244	69,750	86,554	247,700	15
ALL REGIONS	32,000	57,828	76,939	67,441	89,087	247,700	85

State Data

	Min	Q1	Mean	Median	Q3	Max	N
AR	60,000	60,000	65,757	60,000	68,636	77,271	3
CA	57,820	58,040	113,117	98,280	103,746	247,700	5
CO	57,424	58,112	58,341	58,800	58,800	58,800	3
FL	46,514	59,982	77,821	73,450	93,475	113,500	3
GA	50,000	53,092	56,185	56,185	59,277	62,369	2
IN	52,780	52,945	61,034	55,425	63,514	80,504	4
KY	32,000	41,443	54,462	50,885	65,693	80,500	3
LA	50,460	54,595	58,730	58,730	62,865	67,000	2
MA	64,000	68,500	94,074	73,000	109,112	145,223	3
MI	47,800	57,053	66,306	66,306	75,558	84,811	2
MN	63,600	70,074	76,549	76,549	83,023	89,497	2
MO	57,204	66,394	75,585	75,585	84,775	93,965	2
MS	42,500	45,625	48,750	48,750	51,875	55,000	5
ND	69,314	69,518	69,721	69,721	69,925	70,128	2
NE	54,396	63,197	72,215	71,998	81,124	90,250	3
NY	58,000	65,230	92,534	66,232	126,525	140,000	7
OH	50,000	64,250	77,797	80,595	94,142	100,000	4
PA	66,280	76,570	83,014	83,929	90,372	97,917	4
SC	54,000	57,600	66,075	61,200	72,113	83,025	3
TX	50,309	62,655	71,708	75,000	82,408	89,816	3
VA	79,000	90,500	102,000	102,000	113,500	125,000	2
WA	69,750	73,136	76,521	76,521	79,907	83,292	2
WV	48,313	52,117	65,101	55,920	73,495	91,070	3

DIRECTOR/DEAN/CHIEF OFFICER—CONTINUED
University (includes ARL data)

Regional Data

	Min	Q1	Mean	Median	Q3	Max	N
Great Lakes & Plains	70,040	87,578	141,501	144,794	180,634	258,300	26
North Atlantic	71,753	96,007	133,607	116,150	162,500	239,410	28
Southeast	54,075	78,938	128,969	117,624	174,950	250,000	22
West & Southwest	65,000	117,500	138,774	139,900	164,557	212,700	31
ALL REGIONS	54,075	95,014	136,069	134,000	173,099	258,300	107

DIRECTOR/DEAN/CHIEF OFFICER—CONTINUED
ALL ACADEMIC LIBRARIES

Regional Data

	Min	Q1	Mean	Median	Q3	Max	N
Great Lakes & Plains	43,250	65,078	100,660	80,714	130,040	258,300	58
North Atlantic	56,654	73,058	110,925	101,320	134,255	239,410	56
Southeast	32,000	57,898	84,562	68,669	82,013	250,000	83

	Min	Q1	Mean	Median	Q3	Max	N
West & Southwest	42,000	73,250	111,258	101,348	146,011	247,700	58
ALL REGIONS	32,000	64,006	100,852	80,560	129,765	258,300	255

State Data

	Min	Q1	Mean	Median	Q3	Max	N
AL	51,017	63,732	116,135	76,059	175,076	208,252	7
AR	60,000	60,000	68,880	68,636	77,516	78,250	4
AZ	66,000	84,750	124,399	122,901	162,549	185,794	4
CA	57,820	99,761	132,225	109,000	162,950	247,700	11
CO	57,424	58,800	114,091	129,688	142,778	183,288	8
DC	198,977	203,469	207,961	207,961	212,452	216,944	2
FL	46,514	74,588	109,303	95,750	151,375	180,353	6
GA	50,000	58,342	102,436	68,685	108,936	250,000	6
HI	108,000	121,500	135,000	135,000	148,500	162,000	2
IA	52,000	65,280	119,374	80,560	195,845	203,186	5
IL	67,881	81,950	159,832	158,340	232,690	258,300	5
IN	52,000	52,945	73,690	63,425	79,222	145,587	8
KS	43,250	58,823	108,181	92,600	171,610	174,620	5
KY	32,000	46,164	57,489	58,727	70,052	80,500	4
LA	45,000	60,400	73,667	69,000	80,750	138,010	19
MA	64,000	80,097	125,402	131,765	143,931	231,500	8
MD	56,654	61,586	101,472	77,049	107,011	239,410	7
ME	108,851	110,690	129,360	112,528	139,614	166,700	3
MI	47,800	80,867	108,023	84,811	144,000	182,639	5
MN	63,600	68,191	75,293	72,782	81,140	89,497	3
MO	54,346	57,204	82,132	72,000	93,965	153,787	9
MS	42,500	48,750	53,411	55,000	58,867	62,733	6
NC	44,600	57,790	84,576	60,453	86,500	206,000	8
ND	65,010	67,162	68,151	69,314	69,721	70,128	3
NE	54,396	70,040	77,657	71,998	90,250	101,600	5
NM	65,000	69,500	92,967	74,000	106,950	139,900	3
NY	57,766	66,155	108,343	97,896	136,810	236,385	18
OH	50,000	80,595	125,054	100,000	180,096	204,000	7
OK	73,000	74,875	118,818	117,580	161,523	167,113	4
OR	66,890	96,758	126,625	126,625	156,493	186,360	2
PA	66,280	74,655	91,373	80,000	95,473	176,000	11
RI	97,000	105,610	114,221	114,221	122,831	131,441	2
SC	53,667	56,250	66,601	67,100	75,230	83,025	8
TN	54,075	59,925	68,350	64,000	68,418	107,351	8
TX	42,000	68,345	92,026	82,624	116,556	174,588	12
UT	57,784	86,518	124,470	122,048	160,000	196,000	4
VA	79,000	93,276	113,009	111,518	131,250	150,000	4
WA	65,422	71,875	84,043	83,292	87,920	120,000	7
WI	81,836	94,307	106,778	106,778	119,249	131,720	2
WV	48,313	54,018	93,476	73,495	112,953	178,600	4

DEPUTY/ASSOCIATE/ASSISTANT DIRECTOR

Persons who report to the Director and manage major aspects of the library operation (e.g., technical services, public services, collection development, systems/automation).

Two-Year College

Regional Data

	Min	Q1	Mean	Median	Q3	Max	N
Great Lakes & Plains	29,984	43,000	44,670	44,832	47,912	56,052	7
North Atlantic	37,813	61,312	64,966	67,158	72,988	81,191	7
West & Southwest	37,501	43,984	49,823	51,678	53,951	62,000	5
ALL REGIONS	29,984	43,996	53,067	50,573	62,873	81,191	20

State Data

	Min	Q1	Mean	Median	Q3	Max	N
IN	42,000	42,500	43,000	43,000	43,500	44,000	2
MO	44,832	45,594	49,080	46,356	51,204	56,052	3
PA	57,133	65,907	69,491	67,437	75,625	81,191	6
UT	37,501	40,743	44,388	43,984	47,831	51,678	3

DEPUTY/ASSOCIATE/ASSISTANT DIRECTOR—CONTINUED

Four-Year College

Regional Data

	Min	Q1	Mean	Median	Q3	Max	N
Great Lakes & Plains	42,500	46,495	55,861	53,000	65,557	74,282	10
North Atlantic	47,940	61,266	74,597	73,348	82,345	120,487	20
Southeast	36,700	48,247	52,280	49,990	54,487	74,597	14
West & Southwest	48,982	49,522	68,257	56,336	65,650	131,880	7
ALL REGIONS	36,700	49,100	63,621	60,317	73,348	131,880	51

State Data

	Min	Q1	Mean	Median	Q3	Max	N
CA	66,847	83,105	99,364	99,364	115,622	131,880	3
IL	46,959	51,651	56,343	56,343	61,035	65,727	2
IN	45,135	45,436	45,738	45,738	46,039	46,340	2
ME	78,286	79,496	80,707	80,707	81,917	83,127	2
MN	65,046	67,355	69,664	69,664	71,973	74,282	2
MO	42,500	46,625	50,750	50,750	54,875	59,000	2
NY	73,348	77,997	84,226	81,563	85,000	103,221	6
PA	47,940	53,221	59,747	60,317	65,000	70,201	9
SC	49,980	52,283	59,721	54,586	64,592	74,597	3
TX	48,982	49,026	49,070	49,070	49,114	49,158	2
VA	42,128	47,340	49,609	51,059	53,328	54,190	4

DEPUTY/ASSOCIATE/ASSISTANT DIRECTOR—CONTINUED

University (includes ARL data)

Regional Data

	Min	Q1	Mean	Median	Q3	Max	N
Great Lakes & Plains	37,242	77,342	92,704	93,898	107,655	135,951	66
North Atlantic	49,042	81,120	103,446	103,985	127,136	173,354	83
Southeast	47,755	70,178	90,109	86,000	105,000	158,737	57
West & Southwest	55,000	82,000	97,030	93,706	111,624	170,581	77
ALL REGIONS	37,242	77,382	96,509	94,000	114,201	173,354	283

DEPUTY/ASSOCIATE/ASSISTANT DIRECTOR—CONTINUED

ALL ACADEMIC LIBRARIES

Regional Data

	Min	Q1	Mean	Median	Q3	Max	N
Great Lakes & Plains	29,984	65,387	84,214	86,110	103,613	135,951	83
North Atlantic	37,813	69,282	95,946	89,500	120,684	173,354	110
Southeast	36,700	57,660	81,833	77,000	101,675	158,737	73
West & Southwest	37,501	76,916	92,386	91,816	109,742	170,581	89
ALL REGIONS	29,984	67,129	89,381	87,120	108,937	173,354	355

State Data

	Min	Q1	Mean	Median	Q3	Max	N
AL	36,700	80,425	95,524	104,599	119,698	136,197	4
AZ	74,368	77,036	97,817	98,000	109,370	150,000	9
CA	66,847	94,554	114,034	110,205	132,076	170,581	21
CO	82,000	87,556	96,230	93,068	100,720	117,888	9
DC	67,129	95,063	115,605	119,032	140,613	156,921	19
FL	47,755	54,137	70,644	66,679	85,950	105,000	16
GA	44,780	79,125	96,476	101,675	109,839	158,737	15
III	71,256	75,939	79,854	78,000	81,915	92,160	4
IA	78,116	93,501	104,707	100,171	114,057	135,951	12
ID	60,008	60,757	61,506	61,506	62,254	63,003	2
IL	46,959	60,033	84,776	82,404	102,996	130,200	17
IN	42,000	44,568	58,225	46,340	76,065	77,969	7
KS	49,468	77,580	91,394	100,989	106,633	116,280	9
LA	51,519	56,184	60,849	60,849	65,513	70,178	2
MA	58,200	80,831	93,597	88,650	103,488	135,000	22
MD	37,813	83,000	112,614	129,645	133,751	159,563	9
ME	78,286	79,496	80,707	80,707	81,917	83,127	2
MI	29,984	93,273	93,497	100,300	104,375	119,600	8
MN	65,046	67,355	69,664	69,664	71,973	74,282	2
MO	42,500	45,975	63,307	57,298	65,054	115,958	8
NC	76,547	91,170	112,844	119,000	131,590	142,958	10

	Min	Q1	Mean	Median	Q3	Max	N
NM	62,000	68,532	75,063	75,063	81,595	88,126	2
NY	53,000	82,750	104,231	103,742	124,163	173,354	31
OH	47,000	77,263	91,423	86,520	107,995	117,546	13
OK	50,614	64,593	84,647	92,407	97,770	111,624	10
OR	62,058	87,660	96,194	113,262	113,262	113,262	3
PA	47,940	57,133	68,046	65,000	70,201	126,710	25
SC	49,980	52,283	59,721	54,586	64,592	74,597	3
TX	48,982	60,490	82,245	87,801	90,844	138,539	10
UT	37,501	61,500	81,682	84,738	100,017	128,000	18
VA	42,128	52,850	61,727	60,900	71,700	80,000	11
WI	64,589	68,542	73,710	70,620	75,787	89,011	4
WV	42,614	78,857	80,897	83,395	88,447	101,906	9

DEPARTMENT HEAD/COORDINATOR/SENIOR MANAGER

Persons who supervise one or more professional librarians.

Two-Year College

Regional Data

	Min	Q1	Mean	Median	Q3	Max	N
Great Lakes & Plains	37,149	44,467	55,649	47,149	70,346	80,794	6
North Atlantic	30,000	30,000	36,246	30,000	39,369	48,738	4
Southeast	39,100	42,025	56,145	44,000	58,120	97,480	4
West & Southwest	35,000	41,379	46,376	47,310	51,753	56,000	7
ALL REGIONS	30,000	40,404	51,244	45,341	52,848	97,480	22

State Data

	Min	Q1	Mean	Median	Q3	Max	N
AL	97,480	97,480	97,480	97,480	97,480	97,480	1
AZ	56,000	56,000	56,000	56,000	56,000	56,000	2
GA	45,000	45,000	45,000	45,000	45,000	45,000	1
IL	48,616	63,103	69,000	77,589	79,192	80,794	3
KS	37,149	38,877	40,606	40,606	42,334	44,062	2
LA	39,100	40,075	41,050	41,050	42,025	43,000	2
MD	79,423	79,423	79,423	79,423	79,423	79,423	1
MO	45,681	45,681	45,681	45,681	45,681	45,681	1
NY	30,000	30,000	36,246	30,000	39,369	48,738	4
TX	35,000	37,920	42,545	40,839	46,318	51,797	3
UT	43,000	45,155	47,310	47,310	49,464	51,619	2

DEPARTMENT HEAD/COORDINATOR/SENIOR MANAGER—CONTINUED

Four-Year College

Regional Data

	Min	Q1	Mean	Median	Q3	Max	N
Great Lakes & Plains	48,100	49,538	50,975	50,975	52,413	53,850	2

	Min	Q1	Mean	Median	Q3	Max	N
North Atlantic	42,000	58,200	70,697	71,489	81,007	97,627	19
Southeast	27,000	32,771	43,189	40,000	49,940	67,550	18
West & Southwest	37,389	46,257	51,843	51,000	60,000	62,000	8
ALL REGIONS	27,000	42,000	56,452	55,582	67,071	97,627	47

State Data

	Min	Q1	Mean	Median	Q3	Max	N
AR	40,000	40,000	40,000	40,000	40,000	40,000	5
DE	56,000	56,000	56,000	56,000	56,000	56,000	3
KY	27,000	27,000	27,000	27,000	27,000	27,000	1
LA	30,490	32,556	35,224	32,986	39,100	40,990	5
MA	52,020	73,760	78,023	82,713	86,976	94,646	4
ME	55,582	59,559	63,536	63,536	67,512	71,489	2
NC	27,810	27,810	27,810	27,810	27,810	27,810	1
NH	58,200	59,535	69,568	69,870	79,903	80,330	4
NV	60,000	60,000	60,000	60,000	60,000	60,000	2
NY	60,000	61,904	72,198	69,140	79,435	90,513	4
OH	48,100	49,538	50,975	50,975	52,413	53,850	2
SC	47,084	47,084	47,084	47,084	47,084	47,084	1
TX	37,389	44,000	48,580	48,513	51,000	62,000	6
VA	45,000	48,101	51,202	51,202	54,302	57,403	2
VT	42,000	42,000	42,000	42,000	42,000	42,000	1
WV	52,795	59,933	62,472	67,071	67,311	67,550	3

DEPARTMENT HEAD/COORDINATOR/SENIOR MANAGER—CONTINUED

University

Regional Data

	Min	Q1	Mean	Median	Q3	Max	N
Great Lakes & Plains	43,978	54,597	66,508	62,783	79,491	91,720	55
North Atlantic	33,000	56,848	70,167	70,409	82,144	114,792	32
Southeast	41,300	50,265	59,868	61,602	69,456	81,333	37
West & Southwest	50,000	57,251	70,304	68,718	82,452	113,328	44
ALL REGIONS	33,000	54,604	66,892	64,000	78,989	114,792	168

State Data

	Min	Q1	Mean	Median	Q3	Max	N
AL	72,602	73,406	73,961	74,210	74,640	75,070	3
AZ	63,000	63,000	63,000	63,000	63,000	63,000	1
CA	54,000	76,221	82,958	81,900	89,814	113,328	9
CO	51,000	56,091	71,656	71,289	87,895	91,900	6
FL	43,000	50,000	53,720	51,484	62,000	64,000	14
GA	50,353	64,539	67,557	69,271	72,289	81,333	4
HI	56,100	56,201	56,301	56,301	56,402	56,502	5
IL	61,665	70,977	78,272	80,041	84,520	91,720	10

IN	48,000	53,038	56,429	54,328	62,530	64,443	9
KS	45,100	69,719	71,413	77,999	79,976	80,975	10
LA	45,000	45,702	58,984	61,203	69,231	71,700	13
MA	33,000	33,500	41,088	34,000	45,132	56,263	3
MD	49,866	53,685	59,436	57,503	64,221	70,938	3
ME	52,590	59,058	62,102	63,179	63,483	73,695	8
MN	62,660	62,660	62,660	62,660	62,660	62,660	1
MO	43,978	48,489	51,293	53,000	54,950	56,900	4
NE	53,002	55,855	58,024	57,521	59,690	64,050	4
NJ	114,792	114,792	114,792	114,792	114,792	114,792	1
NM	52,300	74,274	75,986	82,606	84,130	86,618	5
NY	71,500	81,027	85,815	83,481	89,804	108,405	12
OH	80,000	83,000	85,314	86,000	87,971	89,942	3
PA	51,646	52,969	60,476	53,166	69,879	74,719	5
TX	50,000	61,292	68,824	69,249	77,719	82,400	11
UT	54,414	56,729	57,854	57,900	59,026	61,202	4
VA	41,300	51,700	57,800	62,100	66,050	70,000	3
WA	53,004	53,187	58,187	53,370	60,779	68,187	3
WI	54,314	54,546	58,302	56,044	61,099	66,579	14

DEPARTMENT HEAD/COORDINATOR/SENIOR MANAGER—CONTINUED
ALL ACADEMIC LIBRARIES

Regional Data

	Min	Q1	Mean	Median	Q3	Max	N
Great Lakes & Plains	37,149	53,856	64,621	62,517	78,989	91,720	63
North Atlantic	30,000	56,000	68,592	69,879	81,338	114,792	56
Southeast	27,000	43,500	54,671	52,061	68,391	97,480	59
West & Southwest	35,000	53,370	65,157	61,000	78,072	113,328	59
ALL REGIONS	27,000	51,759	63,330	61,393	77,653	114,792	237

State Data

	Min	Q1	Mean	Median	Q3	Max	N
AL	72,602	73,808	79,841	74,640	80,673	97,480	4
AR	40,000	40,000	40,000	40,000	40,000	40,000	5
AZ	56,000	57,750	59,500	59,500	61,250	63,000	3
CA	54,000	76,221	82,958	81,900	89,814	113,328	9
CO	51,000	56,091	71,656	71,289	87,895	91,900	6
DE	56,000	56,000	56,000	56,000	56,000	56,000	3
FL	43,000	50,000	53,720	51,484	62,000	64,000	14
GA	45,000	50,353	63,045	69,267	69,274	81,333	5
HI	56,100	56,201	56,301	56,301	56,402	56,502	5
IL	48,616	68,688	76,132	79,032	82,315	91,720	13
IN	48,000	53,038	56,429	54,328	62,530	64,443	9
KS	37,149	47,425	65,251	75,939	79,699	80,975	12

KY	27,000	27,000	27,000	27,000	27,000	27,000	1
LA	30,490	40,518	51,251	45,702	63,210	71,700	20
MA	33,000	43,010	62,194	56,263	82,713	94,646	7
MD	49,866	55,594	64,433	64,221	73,059	79,423	4
ME	52,590	57,715	62,389	63,179	63,920	73,695	10
MN	62,660	62,660	62,660	62,660	62,660	62,660	1
MO	43,978	45,255	49,890	49,341	53,975	56,900	5
NC	27,810	27,810	27,810	27,810	27,810	27,810	1
NE	53,002	55,855	58,024	57,521	59,690	64,050	4
NH	58,200	59,535	69,568	69,870	79,903	80,330	4
NJ	114,792	114,792	114,792	114,792	114,792	114,792	1
NM	52,300	74,274	75,986	82,606	84,130	86,618	5
NV	60,000	60,000	60,000	60,000	60,000	60,000	2
NY	30,000	67,019	75,122	81,338	87,831	108,405	20
OH	48,100	53,850	71,578	80,000	86,000	89,942	5
PA	51,646	52,969	60,476	53,166	69,879	74,719	5
RI	97,627	97,627	97,627	97,627	97,627	97,627	1
SC	47,084	47,084	47,084	47,084	47,084	47,084	1
TX	35,000	49,257	59,348	61,000	70,082	82,400	20
UT	43,000	52,318	54,339	55,957	58,100	61,202	6
VA	41,300	45,000	55,161	57,403	62,100	70,000	5
VT	42,000	42,000	42,000	42,000	42,000	42,000	1
WA	53,004	53,187	58,187	53,370	60,779	68,187	3
WI	54,314	54,546	58,302	56,044	61,099	66,579	14
WV	52,795	59,933	62,472	67,071	67,311	67,550	3

MANAGER/SUPERVISOR OF SUPPORT STAFF

Persons who supervise support staff in any part of the library but do not supervise professional librarians.

Two-Year College

Regional Data

	Min	Q1	Mean	Median	Q3	Max	N
Great Lakes & Plains	45,300	47,000	57,751	48,686	63,250	84,521	6
North Atlantic	43,452	43,644	45,167	43,835	46,025	48,214	3
Southeast	32,000	44,620	54,551	53,864	65,954	76,059	9
West & Southwest	36,300	39,553	45,087	47,226	50,239	52,500	7
ALL REGIONS	32,000	43,452	50,818	48,214	52,500	84,521	25

State Data

	Min	Q1	Mean	Median	Q3	Max	N
AL	58,575	62,946	67,317	67,317	71,688	76,059	3
GA	32,000	34,777	37,555	37,555	40,332	43,109	2
IL	48,686	57,645	66,604	66,604	75,562	84,521	2
IN	47,000	47,000	47,000	47,000	47,000	47,000	2
KY	68,413	68,413	68,413	68,413	68,413	68,413	1

MD	43,452	43,548	43,644	43,644	43,739	43,835	2
MN	63,250	63,250	63,250	63,250	63,250	63,250	1
MO	45,300	45,300	45,300	45,300	45,300	45,300	1
NC	49,152	49,152	49,152	49,152	49,152	49,152	3
PA	48,214	48,214	48,214	48,214	48,214	48,214	1
TX	36,300	36,937	41,261	37,574	43,742	49,909	3
UT	41,532	41,532	41,532	41,532	41,532	41,532	1
WA	47,226	48,897	50,098	50,568	51,534	52,500	3

MANAGER/SUPERVISOR OF SUPPORT STAFF—CONTINUED

Four-Year College

Regional Data

	Min	Q1	Mean	Median	Q3	Max	N
Great Lakes & Plains	36,268	42,925	47,258	46,336	53,096	63,774	17
North Atlantic	50,336	62,275	76,846	69,496	79,684	125,808	16
Southeast	32,800	39,889	45,057	44,055	48,725	60,000	26
West & Southwest	38,061	41,532	51,568	49,244	59,096	77,976	18
ALL REGIONS	32,800	42,376	53,727	47,750	59,700	125,808	77

State Data

	Min	Q1	Mean	Median	Q3	Max	N
AL	45,155	47,103	49,951	49,050	52,349	55,647	3
AR	32,800	35,778	38,805	38,173	38,617	49,939	6
CA	38,061	47,080	56,613	57,325	64,384	77,976	9
CO	38,647	40,184	42,631	41,720	44,624	47,527	3
GA	36,000	36,000	36,000	36,000	36,000	36,000	1
IN	38,550	39,000	48,643	46,123	55,766	63,774	4
KY	43,910	44,910	49,570	45,910	52,400	58,890	3
MA	62,790	67,073	69,704	68,720	71,655	78,835	6
MI	45,000	45,000	45,000	45,000	45,000	45,000	1
MN	45,727	45,879	46,032	46,032	46,184	46,336	2
MO	38,633	42,317	44,309	46,000	47,147	48,293	3
MS	40,365	40,962	41,559	41,559	42,155	42,752	2
NE	47,180	48,678	50,176	50,176	51,674	53,172	2
NY	52,000	64,993	83,621	73,767	101,892	125,808	7
OH	36,268	44,584	48,888	51,321	55,625	56,642	4
OR	52,918	54,202	55,486	55,486	56,770	58,054	2
PA	50,336	51,502	52,668	52,668	53,834	55,000	2
SC	42,000	42,700	43,292	43,400	43,938	44,475	3
TX	39,759	40,061	40,364	40,364	40,666	40,968	2
VA	39,730	43,650	48,888	46,525	54,394	60,000	8
WA	45,000	49,801	54,602	54,602	59,403	64,204	2

MANAGER/SUPERVISOR OF SUPPORT STAFF—CONTINUED

University

Regional Data

	Min	Q1	Mean	Median	Q3	Max	N
Great Lakes & Plains	31,500	46,163	56,923	53,582	64,812	93,393	112
North Atlantic	39,729	48,478	64,232	64,675	72,084	111,089	28
Southeast	40,000	49,042	55,092	54,000	60,000	83,215	51
West & Southwest	35,157	50,213	60,063	56,777	67,452	105,612	70
ALL REGIONS	31,500	48,478	58,678	54,646	65,760	111,089	261

State Data

	Min	Q1	Mean	Median	Q3	Max	N
AL	61,580	61,580	61,580	61,580	61,580	61,580	1
AR	45,570	46,000	46,929	46,547	46,821	49,705	5
AZ	54,000	54,000	54,000	54,000	54,000	54,000	1
CA	49,464	58,363	77,009	78,722	92,305	105,612	9
CO	44,000	50,151	59,983	65,171	68,168	77,333	11
FL	42,848	44,462	51,261	48,097	54,896	66,000	6
GA	43,134	48,036	56,270	59,380	61,518	72,268	7
ID	41,017	43,263	54,319	49,992	61,048	76,275	4
IL	44,525	51,260	65,359	64,769	76,583	92,855	8
IN	45,289	46,467	47,645	47,645	48,822	50,000	2
KS	31,500	46,163	50,506	47,663	57,716	66,625	8
LA	40,000	42,250	44,857	44,715	47,322	50,000	4
MA	46,389	55,769	69,146	67,558	78,077	107,076	8
MD	44,000	46,967	49,934	49,934	52,900	55,867	2
ME	40,900	44,736	50,316	46,182	51,762	67,999	12
MI	46,014	46,636	47,257	47,257	47,879	48,500	18
MN	53,582	53,759	53,936	53,936	54,112	54,289	2
MO	40,388	40,430	43,683	43,172	46,425	48,000	4
NC	47,750	50,032	54,263	53,133	56,944	64,350	6
NE	35,812	35,948	36,084	36,084	36,220	36,356	2
NJ	96,274	99,978	103,682	103,682	107,385	111,089	2
NM	35,157	42,016	47,367	49,001	50,764	60,000	9
NY	48,500	61,643	65,460	66,500	70,928	80,094	8
OH	65,000	67,926	76,415	70,852	82,123	93,393	3
OK	48,852	48,852	48,852	48,852	48,852	48,852	2
PA	39,729	42,265	51,837	51,900	54,000	71,291	5
TN	54,421	56,211	58,378	58,000	60,357	62,713	3
TX	40,750	51,288	56,724	55,200	60,522	81,143	22
UT	50,305	51,260	58,759	59,432	64,031	70,991	7
VA	50,000	53,675	58,934	58,300	60,844	74,800	8
WA	62,500	66,200	72,930	67,327	80,610	89,566	6
WI	47,381	47,381	47,381	47,381	47,381	47,381	1
WV	50,190	53,591	59,338	54,604	61,843	83,215	11

Regional Data

	Min	Q1	Mean	Median	Q3	Max	N
Great Lakes & Plains	31,500	45,900	54,297	50,000	59,350	93,393	135
North Atlantic	39,729	51,118	67,310	65,687	74,115	125,808	47
Southeast	32,000	44,475	51,831	50,000	58,890	83,215	86
West & Southwest	35,157	47,608	57,296	54,000	65,569	105,612	95
ALL REGIONS	31,500	46,097	56,734	53,160	64,350	125,808	363

State Data

	Min	Q1	Mean	Median	Q3	Max	N
AL	45,155	50,699	57,678	57,111	60,829	76,059	7
AR	32,800	38,173	42,497	45,570	46,684	49,939	11
AZ	54,000	54,000	54,000	54,000	54,000	54,000	1
CA	38,061	54,143	67,491	62,220	78,722	105,612	18
CO	38,647	45,632	56,264	51,597	66,913	77,333	14
FL	42,848	44,462	51,261	48,097	54,896	66,000	6
GA	32,000	43,115	50,500	48,036	60,069	72,268	10
ID	41,017	42,515	47,000	44,012	49,992	55,972	3
IL	44,525	50,911	65,608	64,769	77,198	92,855	10
IN	38,550	42,220	48,123	47,000	51,548	63,774	8
KS	31,500	46,163	50,506	47,663	57,716	66,625	8
KY	43,910	45,410	54,281	52,400	61,271	68,413	4
LA	40,000	42,250	44,857	44,715	47,322	50,000	4
MA	46,389	63,514	69,385	68,566	75,957	107,076	14
MD	43,452	43,739	46,789	43,918	46,967	55,867	4
ME	40,900	43,625	51,750	46,350	57,175	67,999	3
MI	45,000	49,728	60,720	54,711	63,157	91,456	82
MN	45,727	46,336	52,637	53,582	54,289	63,250	5
MO	38,633	40,430	44,120	45,600	46,500	48,293	8
MS	40,365	40,962	41,559	41,559	42,155	42,752	2
NC	47,750	49,097	53,533	53,000	55,718	64,350	9
ND	42,925	42,925	42,925	42,925	42,925	42,925	1
NE	35,812	36,220	43,130	41,768	48,678	53,172	4
NJ	96,274	99,978	103,682	103,682	107,385	111,089	2
NM	35,157	42,016	47,367	49,001	50,764	60,000	9
NY	48,500	62,540	73,935	69,256	77,279	125,808	15
OH	36,268	51,321	60,685	56,642	67,926	93,393	7
OK	48,852	48,852	48,852	48,852	48,852	48,852	2
OR	52,918	54,202	55,486	55,486	56,770	58,054	2
PA	39,729	46,727	51,592	51,118	54,250	71,291	8
RI	120,637	120,637	120,637	120,637	120,637	120,637	1
SC	42,000	42,700	43,292	43,400	43,938	44,475	3

SD	54,688	54,688	54,688	54,688	54,688	54,688	1
TN	54,421	56,211	58,378	58,000	60,357	62,713	3
TX	36,300	46,668	53,681	53,294	57,590	81,143	27
UT	41,532	50,925	56,605	55,410	62,016	70,991	8
VA	39,730	47,138	53,911	53,363	59,550	74,800	16
WA	45,000	51,534	63,371	64,204	67,327	89,566	11
WI	47,381	47,381	47,381	47,381	47,381	47,381	1
WV	50,190	53,591	59,338	54,604	61,843	83,215	11

LIBRARIAN WHO DOES NOT SUPERVISE

Full-time staff with master's degrees from programs in library and information studies accredited by the ALA who were not reported earlier and who do not supervise.

Two-Year College

Regional Data

	Min	Q1	Mean	Median	Q3	Max	N
Great Lakes & Plains	36,780	39,000	52,828	51,000	58,602	86,051	10
North Atlantic	34,211	46,221	55,110	56,074	63,168	82,499	25
Southeast	28,499	42,525	48,677	45,000	52,795	90,326	32
West & Southwest	31,568	51,412	55,831	55,559	59,785	94,000	23
ALL REGIONS	28,499	43,072	52,642	51,211	59,014	94,000	90

State Data

	Min	Q1	Mean	Median	Q3	Max	N
CA	85,400	87,550	89,700	89,700	91,850	94,000	2
CT	63,581	63,581	63,581	63,581	63,581	63,581	2
GA	42,000	43,061	43,616	43,105	44,387	45,625	6
IA	52,000	57,750	63,500	63,500	69,250	75,000	3
IL	39,020	39,020	39,020	39,020	39,020	39,020	1
IN	38,000	38,250	38,500	38,500	38,750	39,000	2
KY	55,125	55,125	55,125	55,125	55,125	55,125	2
LA	40,000	40,000	40,000	40,000	40,000	40,000	1
MD	34,211	36,720	42,782	39,654	47,932	55,391	5
MN	51,000	51,000	51,000	51,000	51,000	51,000	1
MO	36,780	36,780	36,780	36,780	36,780	36,780	1
NC	28,499	38,311	40,858	42,498	45,000	50,000	12
NY	44,521	44,559	49,781	47,891	53,113	58,820	5
OH	58,602	65,464	72,327	72,327	79,189	86,051	2
PA	45,650	56,200	61,318	61,410	64,295	82,499	13
SC	44,000	53,677	64,555	59,207	75,500	90,326	7
TN	50,000	50,000	52,500	52,500	55,000	55,000	4
TX	53,689	54,848	57,596	56,007	59,550	63,092	3
UT	31,568	33,865	34,721	36,161	36,298	36,435	3
WA	38,880	52,067	55,084	55,559	58,728	73,807	15

LIBRARIAN WHO DOES NOT SUPERVISE—CONTINUED

Four-Year College

Regional Data

	Min	Q1	Mean	Median	Q3	Max	N
Great Lakes & Plains	22,056	40,031	45,548	45,675	50,173	59,444	35
North Atlantic	35,000	49,339	59,546	57,782	65,017	121,553	49
Southeast	25,986	37,248	42,891	40,700	48,000	82,797	31
West & Southwest	25,000	42,069	53,553	51,250	60,438	98,244	33
ALL REGIONS	22,056	41,720	51,227	49,097	57,348	121,553	148

State Data

	Min	Q1	Mean	Median	Q3	Max	N
AL	28,453	28,453	28,453	28,453	28,453	28,453	1
AR	33,000	33,500	34,000	34,000	34,500	35,000	2
CA	52,700	61,058	74,653	66,548	91,140	98,244	9
CO	29,167	42,000	41,992	42,092	43,000	51,250	9
DE	49,000	49,000	49,000	49,000	49,000	49,000	3
FL	37,160	38,698	50,692	41,405	53,399	82,797	4
GA	44,720	44,720	44,720	44,720	44,720	44,720	1
IL	44,500	44,500	44,500	44,500	44,500	44,500	1
IN	40,000	42,838	43,997	45,675	45,995	46,315	3
KY	42,528	43,896	45,264	45,264	46,632	48,000	2
LA	25,986	29,990	33,993	33,993	37,997	42,000	3
MA	40,000	46,853	55,736	53,841	62,900	76,441	8
ME	56,007	58,631	61,583	62,115	62,757	68,403	5
MI	22,056	28,250	39,105	41,393	46,968	57,092	6
MN	44,906	51,595	53,676	54,273	57,413	59,444	6
MO	37,630	39,347	41,863	39,821	44,097	49,194	6
ND	44,999	45,711	46,424	46,424	47,136	47,848	2
NE	46,476	46,722	48,528	46,968	49,554	52,140	3
NH	58,180	58,190	63,300	58,200	65,860	73,520	3
NY	40,880	53,652	63,226	57,384	65,068	121,553	20
OH	38,000	41,962	46,423	45,925	51,000	55,450	8
OK	25,000	30,497	33,017	35,993	37,026	38,058	3
OR	46,350	48,765	51,181	51,181	53,596	56,011	2
PA	38,400	41,101	44,067	43,802	46,901	50,000	3
RI	42,000	57,769	73,537	73,537	89,306	105,074	6
SC	38,349	40,200	45,164	45,000	50,200	52,000	11
TN	51,266	51,981	52,695	52,695	53,410	54,124	2
TX	38,632	38,632	38,632	38,632	38,632	38,632	1
VA	40,200	40,325	40,450	40,450	40,575	40,700	3
VT	35,000	35,000	35,000	35,000	35,000	35,000	1
WA	45,000	50,920	52,980	53,253	54,907	60,418	9
WV	30,145	31,921	33,697	33,697	35,472	37,248	2

LIBRARIAN WHO DOES NOT SUPERVISE—CONTINUED
University (includes ARL data)

Regional Data

	Min	Q1	Mean	Median	Q3	Max	N
Great Lakes & Plains	32,386	48,335	57,359	54,474	64,129	130,313	526
North Atlantic	33,000	53,184	62,886	60,978	70,933	140,237	355
Southeast	26,353	46,070	55,020	53,423	61,838	100,000	193
West & Southwest	30,347	48,040	59,815	56,312	67,483	114,936	423
ALL REGIONS	26,353	48,866	59,399	56,400	66,516	140,237	1,498

LIBRARIAN WHO DOES NOT SUPERVISE—CONTINUED
ALL ACADEMIC LIBRARIES

Regional Data

	Min	Q1	Mean	Median	Q3	Max	N
Great Lakes & Plains	22,056	47,460	56,027	54,032	62,193	130,313	571
North Atlantic	33,000	52,445	62,145	59,791	69,345	140,237	429
Southeast	25,986	44,260	52,856	50,589	59,604	100,000	256
West & Southwest	25,000	48,000	59,166	55,594	66,367	114,936	480
ALL REGIONS	22,056	47,893	58,263	55,390	65,589	140,237	1,736

State Data

	Min	Q1	Mean	Median	Q3	Max	N
AL	28,453	49,490	57,688	55,295	65,514	96,376	54
AR	33,000	34,000	36,267	35,000	37,900	40,800	3
AZ	43,000	53,324	61,018	60,160	68,481	84,315	44
CA	47,087	64,560	77,315	75,624	92,064	114,936	99
CO	29,167	46,430	54,297	53,062	61,297	91,972	71
CT	63,581	63,581	63,581	63,581	63,581	63,581	2
DC	42,074	58,136	64,926	63,613	70,525	94,042	50
DE	49,000	49,000	49,000	49,000	49,000	49,000	3
FL	26,353	43,575	50,322	49,477	54,519	82,797	46
GA	34,364	44,788	52,329	50,775	58,029	88,353	38
HI	34,848	44,121	60,785	52,992	79,713	103,704	40
IA	45,266	51,837	57,409	55,012	61,825	84,750	48
ID	41,017	43,191	47,008	46,404	47,528	60,195	8
IL	39,020	51,303	62,127	61,250	67,941	130,313	62
IN	38,000	44,609	48,349	45,995	52,607	61,883	23
KS	32,386	46,563	53,916	50,261	59,527	103,920	50
KY	42,528	45,264	48,551	48,000	51,563	55,125	4
LA	25,986	36,250	41,905	41,000	44,056	63,700	7
MA	33,000	53,494	62,969	63,087	71,649	101,570	81
MD	34,211	47,000	56,155	54,151	66,264	80,116	54
ME	40,041	40,900	49,458	47,338	56,663	68,403	18

MI	22,056	48,700	56,813	54,200	67,184	83,413	239
MN	44,906	50,745	52,874	54,003	54,401	59,444	9
MO	36,780	41,960	48,153	47,206	53,528	66,284	39
NC	28,499	45,000	56,456	50,944	65,000	100,000	39
ND	44,999	45,711	46,424	46,424	47,136	47,848	2
NE	35,811	46,968	49,536	47,885	55,539	58,246	9
NH	58,180	58,190	63,300	58,200	65,860	73,520	3
NJ	103,682	106,460	109,237	109,237	112,015	114,792	3
NM	33,976	42,109	51,459	49,934	63,725	76,077	11
NY	40,880	54,998	65,667	61,773	71,929	140,237	143
OH	37,485	52,129	60,023	57,768	70,000	96,272	57
OK	25,000	41,811	49,219	50,895	55,268	65,388	51
OR	41,500	49,667	54,143	52,227	56,853	91,265	28
PA	38,400	50,118	56,208	55,443	60,377	101,500	59
RI	42,000	71,500	76,509	78,000	82,750	105,074	12
SC	38,349	44,250	54,860	50,495	58,596	90,326	18
SD	48,000	52,000	55,508	52,950	59,191	66,933	9
TN	31,000	37,500	45,500	48,695	51,601	55,000	19
TX	38,632	49,454	56,949	55,832	61,648	94,036	57
UT	31,568	43,060	48,857	48,643	53,882	66,404	40
VA	40,000	40,696	53,060	52,850	63,350	74,100	11
VT	35,000	35,000	35,000	35,000	35,000	35,000	1
WA	33,114	49,363	54,066	54,078	56,900	84,884	31
WI	41,336	51,843	53,438	54,887	57,082	59,425	24
WV	30,145	38,569	47,743	44,465	55,025	77,945	17

BEGINNING LIBRARIAN

Full-time staff hired in the last six months with master's degrees from programs in library and information studies accredited by the ALA, but with no professional experience after receiving the degree.

Two-Year College

Regional Data

	Min	Q1	Mean	Median	Q3	Max	N
Great Lakes & Plains	36,000	37,579	39,158	39,158	40,736	42,315	2
Southeast	38,000	40,106	42,621	40,862	44,075	51,000	7
West & Southwest	53,000	53,000	53,000	53,000	53,000	53,000	1
ALL REGIONS	36,000	40,000	43,004	41,300	45,000	53,000	10

State Data

	Min	Q1	Mean	Median	Q3	Max	N
AZ	53,000	53,000	53,000	53,000	53,000	53,000	1
IA	36,000	36,000	36,000	36,000	36,000	36,000	1
IL	42,315	42,315	42,315	42,315	42,315	42,315	1
MS	40,424	40,424	40,424	40,424	40,424	40,424	1

	Min	Q1	Mean	Median	Q3	Max	N
SC	38,000	40,000	43,060	41,300	45,000	51,000	6
TN	41,300	41,300	41,300	41,300	41,300	41,300	2

BEGINNING LIBRARIAN—CONTINUED
Four-Year College

Regional Data

	Min	Q1	Mean	Median	Q3	Max	N
Great Lakes & Plains	34,475	36,275	39,328	39,000	42,000	44,892	6
North Atlantic	32,944	38,125	43,986	43,737	50,119	55,000	7
Southeast	37,000	37,375	43,684	38,574	44,883	60,588	5
West & Southwest	35,000	38,500	41,435	41,500	42,000	50,173	5
ALL REGIONS	32,944	37,375	42,123	39,824	45,538	60,588	23

State Data

	Min	Q1	Mean	Median	Q3	Max	N
CA	42,000	42,000	42,000	42,000	42,000	42,000	1
FL	37,000	42,897	48,794	48,794	54,691	60,588	3
IA	42,000	42,000	42,000	42,000	42,000	42,000	2
IN	34,475	35,375	36,583	36,275	37,638	39,000	3
KY	39,648	39,648	39,648	39,648	39,648	39,648	1
MA	47,474	47,474	47,474	47,474	47,474	47,474	1
ME	40,000	40,000	40,000	40,000	40,000	40,000	1
MS	37,500	37,500	37,500	37,500	37,500	37,500	1
NE	44,892	44,892	44,892	44,892	44,892	44,892	1
NY	32,944	41,972	46,315	51,000	53,000	55,000	4
OK	35,000	35,000	35,000	35,000	35,000	35,000	1
OR	41,500	41,500	41,500	41,500	41,500	41,500	1
PA	37,500	37,500	37,500	37,500	37,500	37,500	1
TX	38,500	38,500	38,500	38,500	38,500	38,500	1
WA	50,173	50,173	50,173	50,173	50,173	50,173	1

BEGINNING LIBRARIAN—CONTINUED
University (includes ARL data)

Regional Data

	Min	Q1	Mean	Median	Q3	Max	N
Great Lakes & Plains	29,500	38,451	43,140	43,500	48,750	55,640	17
North Atlantic	30,000	40,000	50,284	50,750	60,589	67,004	19
Southeast	28,514	42,000	46,495	46,350	51,500	63,000	30
West & Southwest	30,014	40,500	46,870	43,000	47,000	82,392	20
ALL REGIONS	28,514	40,000	46,817	45,000	52,000	82,392	86

ALL ACADEMIC LIBRARIES

Regional Data

	Min	Q1	Mean	Median	Q3	Max	N
Great Lakes & Plains	29,500	36,432	41,911	41,004	45,844	55,640	25
North Atlantic	30,000	39,750	48,710	49,500	56,250	67,004	26
Southeast	28,514	39,824	45,510	45,000	50,500	63,000	42
West & Southwest	30,014	40,000	45,868	42,492	48,500	82,392	26
ALL REGIONS	28,514	39,000	45,560	43,132	51,000	82,392	119

State Data

	Min	Q1	Mean	Median	Q3	Max	N
AL	42,000	42,000	42,000	42,000	42,000	42,000	2
AZ	40,000	45,750	48,167	51,500	52,250	53,000	5
CA	42,000	42,000	42,000	42,000	42,000	42,000	3
CO	45,500	45,500	45,500	45,500	45,500	45,500	1
DC	51,500	52,205	56,923	56,220	60,938	63,753	4
FL	37,000	39,750	46,750	45,675	51,758	60,588	7
GA	28,514	43,250	48,736	48,000	57,380	62,100	11
HI	42,492	52,467	62,442	62,442	72,417	82,392	2
IA	36,000	39,000	40,500	42,000	42,750	43,500	4
ID	30,014	33,264	36,514	36,514	39,764	43,014	3
IL	42,315	47,658	50,318	53,000	54,320	55,640	3
IN	34,475	35,375	36,583	36,275	37,638	39,000	3
KS	29,500	37,250	40,208	45,000	45,563	46,125	3
KY	39,648	39,648	39,648	39,648	39,648	39,648	1
LA	35,000	40,000	42,333	45,000	46,000	47,000	4
MA	30,000	42,750	47,694	47,237	52,181	66,300	5
ME	38,500	38,875	39,250	39,250	39,625	40,000	2
MI	34,919	35,911	39,774	36,902	42,201	47,500	5
MO	40,000	40,000	40,003	40,000	40,004	40,008	3
MS	37,500	38,231	38,962	38,962	39,693	40,424	2
NC	50,000	50,000	53,750	51,000	54,750	63,000	4
NE	33,000	35,973	38,946	38,946	41,919	44,892	2
NY	32,944	40,000	48,813	50,000	55,000	67,004	14
OK	35,000	37,065	39,130	39,130	41,195	43,260	2
OR	41,500	41,500	41,500	41,500	41,500	41,500	1
PA	37,500	37,500	37,500	37,500	37,500	37,500	1
SC	38,000	39,500	43,500	42,500	46,500	51,000	4
SD	52,000	52,000	52,000	52,000	52,000	52,000	1
TN	37,853	38,927	39,718	40,000	40,650	41,300	6
TX	38,500	41,000	43,500	43,500	46,000	48,500	2
UT	36,500	39,000	46,876	41,000	43,000	74,880	6

WA	50,173	50,173	50,173	50,173	50,173	50,173	1
WV	37,000	37,000	37,000	37,000	37,000	37,000	1

Discussion

Summary of Results

People interested in a particular type of library, a particular type of work or a particular region will have their own way of drawing conclusion from the results of this survey. However, the results may be summarized in a very general way by noting that this survey included 11,315 individual salaries from 618 libraries, ranging from $22,000 to $258,300 with a mean of $61,072 ($60,734 in 2010, an increase of less than 1 percent) and a median of $56,760 ($55,883 in 2010, an increase of 2 percent). It may be useful to look at mean and median salaries paid to particular types of positions and paid by particular types of libraries, and mean and median salaries paid in particular geographic areas of the United States. All of the data, since 2006, from the ALA-APA Salary Survey: Librarian— Public and Academic (Librarian) and ALA-APA Salary Survey: Non-MLS—Public and Academic (Non-MLS) are included in the ALA-APA Library Salary Database. Visit http://ala-apa.org/files/2012/02/SalarySurveySubscriptionForm.pdf for subscription information.

Salaries by Type of Position

The six positions are shown in Table 1 by position and mean of salaries paid in Public and academic Libraries, comparing 2010 and 2012. Tables 2 and 3 compare the difference in mean salaries from 2010 to 2012 for the six positions by library category. Mean salaries for Director and Beginning Librarian were lower this year, while Deputy/Associate/Assistant Director increased the most (about 8 percent) compared with the others. The highest actual salary reported in 2012 was $258,300 and no high outliers were removed.

Data presented in the academic salary tables for the six categories are distinguished as follows:

- Director/Dean/Chief Officer—includes Association of Research Libraries member data (ARL)
- Deputy/Associate/Assistant Director— includes ARL
- Department Head/Branch Manager/ Coordinator/Senior Manager
- Manager/Supervisor of Support Staff
- Librarian Who Does Not Supervise—includes ARL
- Beginning Librarian—includes ARL

Data presented in the academic libraries tables for the six positions are distinguished by type of library as follows:

- Two-Year College
- Four-Year College
- University (including Association of Research Libraries members)

Data presented in the public libraries tables for the same six positions are distinguished by population served as follows:

Table 1: Position Types by Mean of Salaries Paid, Comparison 2010 and 2012

	COMBINED Regional Salary Data			
	2010	2012	Difference	N
Director/Dean/Chief Officer	99,176	98,213	-963	587
Deputy/Associate/Assistant Director	79,274	85,609	6,335	726
Dept. Head/Branch Manager/Coordinator/ Sr. Manager	65,829	66,606	777	2,758
Manager/Supervisor of Support Staff	55,055	56,033	978	1,478
Librarian Who Does Not Supervise	53,923	55,474	1,551	5,044
Beginning Librarian	48,317	45,660	-2,657	722
Total				11,315

- Very Small—serving less than 10,000
- Small—serving 10,000–24,999
- Medium—serving 25,000–99,999
- Large—serving 100,000–499,999
- Very large—serving 500,000 or more

Salaries Reported

All salaries above $22,000 are reported. At the 2007 American Library Association Midwinter Meeting in Seattle, Washington, the ALA-APA Council voted to approve a Nonbinding Minimum Salary for Professional Librarians of $40,000 (see Appendix E). In 2010 as in 2012, salaries reported did not reach that level in all areas of the country. Tables 4 through 7—Highest Mean, Lowest Mean, Highest Actual and Lowest Actual—illustrate the range of salaries commanded by librarians with an ALA accredited Master's Degree (ALA MLS). The minimum salary of $40,000 was promoted as a vehicle to assist in salary improvement efforts for librarians in small, rural and poorly-funded libraries and to establish a baseline for salaries for beginning librarians. The minimum salary and the ALA-APA Better Salaries and Pay Equity Toolkit (http://ala-apa.org/files/2012/05/toolkit.pdf) are tools that have been successfully used to increase salaries for librarians.

Highest Mean Salaries Reported

Directors of University (including Association of Research Libraries members), Very Large and Large public libraries earned the highest mean salaries, which is typical. In 2012, there were 13 mean salaries above $100,000 (11 in 2010), of which ten are shown in Table 4; there were 20 median salaries above $100,000. The salaries are arrayed high to low by mean. Director salaries over $100,000 were 63 percent of all Director positions reported—65 percent public library Directors and 60 percent of academic.

Lowest Mean Salaries Reported

The lowest mean salaries reported were found across all regions and primarily in 4-year

Table 2. Position Types by Mean of Salaries Paid, Public Libraries, Comparison 2010 and 2012

	Public Regional Salary Data			
	2010	2012	Difference	N
Director/Dean/Chief Officer	100,106	96,187	-3,919	332
Deputy/Associate/Assistant Director	77,633	80,044	2,411	371
Dept. Head/Branch Manager/Coordinator/Sr. Manager	65,875	63,531	-2,344	2,521
Manager/Supervisor of Support Staff	54,863	53,877	-986	1,115
Librarian Who Does Not Supervise	52,851	50,276	-2,575	3,305
Beginning Librarian	48,749	46,168	-2,581	603
Total				8,247

Table 3. Position Types by Mean of Salaries Paid, Academic Libraries, Comparison 2010 and 2012

	Academic Regional Salary Data			
	2010	2012	Difference	N
Director/Dean/Chief Officer	97,767	100,852	3,085	255
Deputy/Associate/Assistant Director	81,897	90,934	9,037	355
Dept. Head/Branch Manager/Coordinator/Sr. Manager	65,320	66,895	1,575	237
Manager/Supervisor of Support Staff	57,079	56,734	-345	363
Librarian Who Does Not Supervise	55,732	58,209	2,477	1,739
Beginning Librarian	47,000	45,560	-1,440	119
Total				3,068

colleges or smaller public libraries, as shown in Table 5. In 2012, there were 11 mean and 14 median salaries below the $40,000 ALA recommended minimum salary. The salaries are arrayed from low to high by mean. The only positions not represented in this table are Director and Manager/Supervisor of Support Staff.

Highest Actual Salaries Reported

There were 23 salaries reported above $180,000 in 2010; in 2012, there were 27. All were Directors. The ten highest salaries are reported in Table 6. The highest salary earners were primarily in University libraries.

Lowest Actual Salaries Reported

There were 34 salaries reported below $22,000, which were removed from the sample in keeping with a long-standing practice of the Librarian Salary Survey. With these salaries excluded, there were 595 actual salaries (8 percent of the total number of salaries submitted, eight percent in 2012) below the $40,000 minimum recommended by ALA-APA; and 23 that were exactly $40,000. The lowest five actual salaries are listed in Table 7 and represent 103 reported salaries. There was some variety in the positions, types of libraries and regions where the lowest salaries were reported. Note that the N or number of employees for these salaries is substantial for entries 3 and 4, about 3 percent of total responses for this position.

Complicating Factors

There were several complications as a result of the change in sampling methodology briefly discussed in the Introduction and Results sections.

Response Rate

Non-Responses

This salary survey also shares many of the complicating factors that will always be associated with conducting a salary survey of librarians:

- The Meaning of "Full-Time"
- The Meaning of "Professional" and "ALA-accredited master's degrees"

These complications are discussed at length below.

Response Rate

The sample of libraries invited to participate in the survey was nominally reduced to 1,669 from 1,672 in 2012. There were 1,005 public and 664 academic libraries. In 2006, the sample was increased to capture and report region- and state-level data, but it was determined this year that a smaller sample would yield adequate results. We continue our efforts to supply the library community with more comprehensive national and state-level salary data both for managers developing budgets and salary ranges and also for job seekers. Although the overall response rates for some regions and states were too low to be statistically

Table 4. Highest Mean and Median Salaries Reported

	Position	Region	Library Type	Mean	Median	N
1	Director/Dean/Chief Officer	North Atlantic	University	207,961	207,961	2
2	Director/Dean/Chief Officer	Great Lakes & Plains	University	199,516	199,516	2
3	Director/Dean/Chief Officer	Great Lakes & Plains	University	188,064	190,000	3
4	Director/Dean/Chief Officer	North Atlantic	Very Large Public	188,000	188,000	1
5	Director/Dean/Chief Officer	West & Southwest	University	186,360	186,360	1
6	Director/Dean/Chief Officer	Southeast	University	186,134	188,001	3
7	Director/Dean/Chief Officer	Southeast	University	185,124	185,124	2
8	Director/Dean/Chief Officer	Great Lakes & Plains	University	182,820	195,515	4
9	Director/Dean/Chief Officer	Southeast	University	178,600	178,600	1
10	Director/Dean/Chief Officer	North Atlantic	Large Public	175,000	175,000	1

significant, all of the data are reported and readers are encouraged to be conscious of the number of responses when using the data.

The response rate was higher in 2012, at 37 percent, thanks to state library data coordinators, and others encouraging library staff to respond. Table 8 shows response rates over the last 12 years.

Please note that the response rate was from Small Public Libraries and Four-Year College

Table 5. Lowest Mean and Median Salaries Reported

	Position	Region	Library Type	Mean	Median	N
1	Librarian Who Does Not Supervise	Southeast	Four-Year College	28,453	28,453	1
2	Department Head/Coordinator/ Senior Manager	Southeast	Four-Year College	27,810	27,810	1
3	Department Head/Coordinator/ Senior Manager	Southeast	Medium Public	27,488	27,488	1
4	Librarian Who Does Not Supervise	Great Lakes & Plains	Small Public	27,123	27,123	1
5	Department Head/Coordinator/ Senior Manager	Southeast	Four-Year College	27,000	27,000	1
6	Beginning Librarian	Great Lakes & Plains	Medium Public	26,972	26,972	1
7	Beginning Librarian	North Atlantic	Very Small Public	24,115	24,115	1
8	Dept. Head/Branch Manager/ Coordinator/Sr. Manager	North Atlantic	Very Small Public	24,100	24,115	3
9	Beginning Librarian	Southeast	Large Public	23,500	23,500	3
10	Manager/Supervisor of Support Staff	North Atlantic	Very Small Public	23,036	23,036	1

Table 6. Highest Actual Salaries Reported

	Position	Region	Library Type	Maximum Salary Reported ($)
1	Director/Dean/Chief Officer	Great Lakes & Plains	University	258,300
2	Director/Dean/Chief Officer	Southeast	University	250,000
3	Director/Dean/Chief Officer	West & Southwest	Four-Year	247,700
4	Director/Dean/Chief Officer	North Atlantic	University	239,410
5	Director/Dean/Chief Officer	North Atlantic	University	236,385
6	Director/Dean/Chief Officer	North Atlantic	University	231,500
7	Director/Dean/Chief Officer	North Atlantic	University	216,944
8	Director/Dean/Chief Officer	West & Southwest	University	212,700
9	Director/Dean/Chief Officer	West & Southwest	Very Large Public	212,345
10	Director/Dean/Chief Officer	Southeast	University	208,252

Table 7. Lowest Actual Salaries Reported

	Position	Region	Library Type	Minimum Salary Reported	N
1	Beginning Librarian	Southeast	Large Public	22,000	3
2	Librarian Who Does Not Supervise	Great Lakes & Plains	Four-Year College	22,056	6
3	Librarian Who Does Not Supervise	Southeast	Large Public	22,335	46
4	Librarian Who Does Not Supervise	North Atlantic	Very Small Public	22,477	3
5	Librarian Who Does Not Supervise	Great Lakes & Plains	Medium Public	22,658	45

Libraries were low at 26 percent. Response rates for Medium-Sized and Very-Small Public Libraries also were low at 30 and 31 percent, respectively. Appendix B, Tables B-2 through B-10, show the participation rate by library type and region.

A selection of the 123 members of the Association of Research Libraries (ARL) was asked for permission to use the salary data they had already provided to ARL. Of the 123, 44 were invited and 33 (75 percent) granted

permission to use their data for the four positions listed above as "includes Association of Research Libraries member data (ARL)." The response from ARL members was 3 points higher this year. To alleviate confusion for respondents, the survey Web page listed ARL members and led those members to a specific web page. ARL members also were sent a different letter, which requested permission (see Appendix C).

Table 8: Response Rates, 2000 through 2012

Year and Survey	Sample	Responses	Response Rate (%)
2012—Librarian	1,669	618	37
2010—Librarian	1,672	583	35
2009—Librarian	3,590	1,179	33
2008—Librarian	3,484	1,010	29
2007—Librarian and Non-MLS combined	3,484	834	24
2006—Librarian	3,418	1,053	31
2006—Non-MLS	3,418	836	24
2005—Librarian	4,343	2,058	47
2004—Librarian	1,275	881	69
2003—Librarian	1,268	901	72
2002—Librarian	1,320	924	70
2001—Librarian	1,297	866	67
2000—Librarian	1,294	931	72

Table 9. Positions by Region and Library Type for Which No Data Was Received

Position	Region	Library Type
Director/Dean/Chief Officer	Southeast	Very Small Public
Director/Dean/Chief Officer	West & Southwest	Very Small Public
Deputy/Associate/Assistant Director	Southeast	Very Small Public
Deputy/Associate/Assistant Director	West & Southwest	Very Small Public
Department Head/Coordinator/Senior Manager	Southeast	Very Small Public
Department Head/Coordinator/Senior Manager	West & Southwest	Very Small Public
Manager/Supervisor of Support Staff	Southeast	Very Small Public
Manager/Supervisor of Support Staff	West & Southwest	Very Small Public
Manager/Supervisor of Support Staff	Southeast	Small Public
Librarian Who Does Not Supervise	Southeast	Very Small Public
Librarian Who Does Not Supervise	West & Southwest	Very Small Public
Beginning Librarian	Great Lakes & Plains	Very Small Public
Beginning Librarian	Southeast	Very Small Public
Beginning Librarian	West & Southwest	Very Small Public
Beginning Librarian	West & Southwest	Small Public
Beginning Librarian	North Atlantic	Two-Year College

Non-Responses

In total, 63 percent of libraries sampled did not respond to the survey. However, the 37 percent response rate is satisfactory for a national survey. No data was received for the positions, regions and library types identified in Table 9.

The Meaning of "Full-Time"

The questionnaire asked about salaries for full-time and part-time incumbents. Smaller libraries depend on part-time staff at all levels, and it is not unusual for staff in librarian positions to be part-time. If no hours were designated, 40 hours was assumed. All salaries were converted to full-time salaries, based on a 40-hour work week, for the purposes of analysis. The months in a year problem affects academic and public libraries where librarians sometimes have contracts for less than twelve months or the number of hours considered to be full-time may be anywhere between 30 and 40 hours. In the survey, all salaries are treated as full-time salaries, regardless of the number of months or hours actually worked.

The Meaning of "Professional" and "ALA Accredited Master's Degrees"

Who is a librarian? This is not a simple question. In smaller, rural and branch public libraries, the director may not have a Master's degree in Library and/or Information Science and/or Studies. ALA policy 54.2 Librarians: Appropriate Degrees states, "The master's degree from a program accredited by the American Library Association (or from a master's level program in library and information studies accredited or recognized by the appropriate national body of another country) is the appropriate professional degree for librarians." For this survey, we asked respondents in libraries with three or more staff members to report only staff with master's degrees from programs in library and information studies (MLS) accredited by American Library Association (ALA). In past surveys, we have asked the respondent to make a decision based on the definition in ALA's statement on "Library and Information Studies Education and Human Resource Utilization"—(www.ala.org/ala/aboutala/offices/hrdr/educprofdev/lepu.pdf).

Appendix A. Survey Questionnaire

2012 ALA-APA LIBRARIAN SALARY SURVEY
Completed Survey due March 1, 2012

Questionnaire completed by:	
Phone (include area code)	
Ext.	
E-Mail Address	

Job Code (see Job Descriptions pdf)	Job Title (see Job Descriptions pdf)	Actual Base Salary (no averages)	# Employees at this rate
Job Code (see Job	Job Title (see Job Descriptions pdf)	Actual Base Salary	#

Completed Survey due March 1, 2012

Descriptions pdf)		(no averages)	Employees at this rate

Supplemental Questions

2012 ALA-APA LIBRARIAN SALARY SURVEY

Completed Survey due March 1, 2012

Has the current economic downturn affected your library's spending on professional development for staff?	
Has the current economic downturn affected your library's spending on recruitment?	

Has the current economic downturn affected your library's recruitment efforts in any of the following ways?

Recruiting for vacancies only	
Recruiting for newly formed positions	
Recruiting in all departments	
Recruiting in some departments, but not all departments	

Has the current economic downturn resulted in changes in library services?

An increase in library services	
A decrease in library services	
An increase in services to particular audiences	
A decrease to services to particular audiences	

Do any librarian staff positions require bilingual or multi-lingual skills?

Do any librarian staff positions require bilingual or multi-lingual skills?	
Collection development staff	
Liasions to non-English speaking patrons	
Staff that provide literacy or library skills training for library patrons	
Staff that provide reference assistance	
Staff that provide technology training for library patrons	
Staff that provide public programs	

Which of your library's employees are covered by a collective bargaining agreement?

Librarians	
Other Professional Staff	
Support Staff	

Which compensation strategies do you use in your current pay system?

Cost of Living Allowances (COLA)	
Scale plus Cost of Living Allowances (COLA)	
Cash Incentives	
Bonuses (Variable Pay)	
Broadbanding	
Job-based or Skill-based Pay	
Merit Pay	
Other Pay Options (Please list)	

What additional forms of compensation do you provide?

Award Programs	

2012 ALA-APA LIBRARIAN SALARY SURVEY

Completed Survey due March 1, 2012

Compensatory Time	
Conference Atttendance	
Membership Dues	
Sabbaticals	
Team-based Pay	
Other (Please list)	

Appendix B. Methodology

Formation of Library Groups

As in previous years, the survey samples were selected from two library universes—public and academic. The public library universe included all public libraries and was stratified into five classes using the 2009 public library file: Very Small, serving populations less than 10,000; Small, serving 10,000–24,999; Medium, serving 25,000–99,999; Large, serving 100,000–499,999; and Very Large, serving 500,000 or more.

The academic library universe was stratified into three categories: Two-Year college, Four-Year college and University (including Association of Research Libraries members' data) using the 2010 Academic Library Survey file (the most current and complete file available). This file includes codes for the categories created by the Carnegie Foundation for the Advancement of Teaching in 1994. Our "Two-Year college" corresponds to the Carnegie category "Associate of Arts." Our "Four-Year college" category corresponds to the Carnegie Categories "Baccalaureate I and II." Our "University" includes the Carnegie categories "Master's I and II, Doctoral I and II, and Research I and II."

Sample Selection and Return

The sample frame for each type/size/geographic strata was determined by applying a proportional sampling procedure for each population category (unduplicated population served or student full-time enrollment) and a 95 percent confidence interval, +/- 5 percent. The public library sample was selected using the Public Library (Public Use) Data File, Fiscal Year 2009 reported by state library agencies as part of the Institute of Museum and Library Services Library Statistics Program.[1] The file includes data on all ALA-accredited and non-ALA

accredited MLS and other staff. Surveys were sent to a sample of libraries that had at least two full-time equivalent (FTE) staff members with an ALA-accredited master's degree (MLS). The proportional random sample was based on how libraries in the determined population served ranges parsed in the universe data file. One-third of each category was randomly identified, except in Large one-half and Very Large all were selected. The ranges in the FY2009 universe file were Very Small (8 percent), Small (27 percent), Medium (45 percent), Large (17 percent), and Very Large (3 percent). One thousand and five (1,005) public libraries were surveyed.

The procedure for selecting the academic library sample followed that used for public libraries, a proportional random sample. The ALA created a sampling frame using the 2010 National Center for Education Statistics (NCES) data files Academic Libraries: 2010, including libraries with two or more staff—reported as "Librarian" and using a 95% confidence interval, +/-5 percent.[2] Then, one-third of the sample was randomly selected. Excluded from the universe file prior to drawing the proportional random sample were institutions categorized as "specialized" by the Carnegie Corporation for the Advancement of Teaching. Those institutions offer degrees ranging from the bachelor's to the doctorate, at least 50 percent of which are in a single specialized field, e.g., "theological seminaries, Bible colleges and other institutions offering degrees in religion," and "Schools of art, music and design." Specialized institutions often declined to respond in the early years of this survey. Also excluded were four sets of institutions whose individual members had been unable to respond in the past. In New York, the seventeen institutions that are part of the City University of New York were removed because librarians there have full academic status and salary is not

1. Miller, K., Henderson, E., Craig, T., Dorinski, S., Freeman M., Isaac, N., Keng, J., McKenzie, L., O'Shea, P., Ramsey, C., Sheckells, C. (2009). Data File Documentation: Public Libraries Survey: Fiscal Year 2009 (IMLS-2009–PLS-01). Institute of Museum and Library Services. Washington, DC.

2. The academic libraries sample was drawn from the National Center for Education Statistics Academic Library Data File, Public-Use: 2010 http://nces.ed.gov/surveys/libraries/aca_data.asp.

related to position description. Public Two-Year colleges in California were removed for the same reason, as were the fourteen members of the state university system in Pennsylvania. Also in Pennsylvania, ALA removed all but the main campus of Pennsylvania State University because librarians at other campuses declined to respond in the past and referred us to the main campus. Six hundred and four (664) academic libraries were surveyed.

The universe of libraries meeting the staffing criteria was 2,628 public and 2,013 academic libraries, necessitating an overall sample of 1,669 to ensure a fifty percent response rate. A total of 1,669 surveys were sent and responses from a total of 583 libraries reporting for 11,554 positions were analyzed for this report. Three of the responding academic libraries requested to be included in the survey without invitation and completed the survey voluntarily.

Procedure

The cover letter was mailed in January 2012 to academic and public libraries with directions for participating online, or participating by downloading and printing a paper survey. A separate letter was sent to Association of Research Libraries (ARL) members asking for permission to use their data.

Respondents could complete the survey in several ways: through a secure website or on a pdf worksheet that could be faxed or emailed to Counting Opinions (SQUIRE) Ltd. The ARL and all but the largest public libraries (serving 500,000 or more) completed the survey electronically via the established website. A reminder letter was sent to all non-respondents in March, reminding them of the deadline of February 29, 2012.

The web survey closed on March 30, and all responses were cleaned and analyzed using LibPAS.

Table B-1. States In Four Regions of the U.S.

North Atlantic	Great Lakes & Plains	Southeast	West & Southwest
Connecticut	Illinois	Alabama	Alaska
Delaware	Indiana	Arkansas	Arizona
District of Columbia	Iowa	Florida	California
Maine	Kansas	Georgia	Colorado
Maryland	Michigan	Kentucky	Hawaii
Massachusetts	Minnesota	Louisiana	Idaho
New Hampshire	Missouri	Mississippi	Montana
New Jersey	Nebraska	North Carolina	Nevada
New York	North Dakota	South Carolina	New Mexico
Pennsylvania	Ohio	Tennessee	Oklahoma
Rhode Island	South Dakota	Virginia	Oregon
Vermont	Wisconsin	West Virginia	Texas
			Utah
			Washington
			Wyoming

Source: *Statistics of Public Libraries, 1977–1978* (NCES, 1982)

Table B-2. Very Large Public Libraries: Size of Sample, Return

	Sample	Return	
		#	% of Sample
North Atlantic	13	8	62
Great Lakes & Plains	10	7	70
Southeast	21	12	57
West & Southwest	39	21	54
TOTAL	83	48	58

Table B-3. Large Public Libraries: Size of Sample, Return

	Sample	Return	
		#	% of Sample
North Atlantic	30	12	40
Great Lakes & Plains	49	24	49
Southeast	72	32	44
West & Southwest	71	37	52
TOTAL	222	105	47

ARL Libraries

ARL Libraries were asked for permission to use the ARL data for positions that closely match ALA-APA ALA MLS survey positions. The codes used were DIRLIB, ASCDIR, ASTDIR, PUBS, TECH, ADMIN, REF and CAT.

Table B-4. Medium-Sized Public Libraries: Size of Sample, Return

	Sample	Return	
		#	% of Sample
North Atlantic	128	36	28
Great Lakes & Plains	119	36	30
Southeast	74	15	20
West & Southwest	71	31	44
TOTAL	392	118	30

Table B-5. Small Public Libraries: Size of Sample, Return

	Sample	Return	
		#	% of Sample
North Atlantic	127	35	28
Great Lakes & Plains	68	14	21
Southeast	12	3	25
West & Southwest	29	9	31
TOTAL	236	61	26

Table B-6. Very Small Public Libraries: Size of Sample, Return

	Sample	Return	
		#	% of Sample
North Atlantic	40	13	33
Great Lakes & Plains	23	8	35
Southeast	2	1	50
West & Southwest	7	0	0
TOTAL	72	22	31

Table B-7. Two-Year College Libraries: Size of Sample, Return

	Sample	Return	
		#	% of Sample
North Atlantic	47	15	32
Great Lakes & Plains	46	20	43
Southeast	61	26	43
West & Southwest	41	18	44
TOTAL	195	79	41

Large and Very Large Public Libraries

Large and Very Large public libraries were mailed a copy of the questionnaire, but also were given the option of participating online, using MS Excel spreadsheets or returning their paper survey to The Association. Fourteen Very Large public libraries took advantage of the MS Excel option. Data from paper surveys received at The Association were entered online by Association staff.

Table B-8. Four-Year College Libraries: Size of Sample, Return

	Sample	Return	
		#	% of Sample
North Atlantic	67	13	19
Great Lakes & Plains	60	18	30
Southeast	72	22	31
West & Southwest	38	8	21
TOTAL	237	61	26

Table B-9. University and ARL Libraries: Size of Sample, Return

	Sample	Return	
		#	% of Sample
North Atlantic	67	33	49
Great Lakes & Plains	52	27	52
Southeast	56	25	45
West & Southwest	57	39	68
TOTAL	232	124	53

Table B-10. All Libraries Surveyed: Size of Sample, Return

	Sample	Return	
		#	% of Sample
North Atlantic	519	165	32
Great Lakes & Plains	427	154	36
Southeast	370	136	37
West & Southwest	353	163	46
TOTAL	1,669	618	37

Appendix C. Cover Letter

For Online Participation:
http://www.alasurveys.org/olstart/olsite/index.cfm
UserID:
Password: (case sensitive)

Dear Colleague:

You are invited to participate in the annual *ALA-APA Library Salary Survey—Librarians: Public and Academic.* **For 2010, we are collecting salary data for six librarian titles.** Your library is one of a scientifically selected sample and your response is critical. For those of you who are unfamiliar with the Librarian Salary Survey, it provides the library community with sound salary data by state, region, library size, and type. Though we appreciate the time this takes, please help us attain a 50% response rate. **The deadline is February 26, 2010.**

All responding institutions receive the benefit of 25% off the print price of the Librarian Salary Survey. **In addition, we will give responding institutions that** *provide contact information* **a discount subscription to the** *Library Salary Database,* **which includes librarian and non-MLS salaries from 2006 to the present.** The ALA-APA Library Salary Database allows users to run reports on more than 65 library positions in academic and public libraries by library type, state and region.

The survey is being conducted online with the assistance of The Management Association of Illinois. Your library has a unique identifier to access the survey (noted at the top of this letter). You may also participate via downloading a MS Excel spreadsheet or completing the questionnaire. The instructions and Web address are on the enclosed instruction page. Libraries that participated via Excel spreadsheet in 2009 may receive a copy of their 2009 spreadsheet file upon request.

> **The supplemental questions for 2010 will focus on compensation strategies and collective bargaining to update 2005 data.**

We want this to be a successful survey and will work with you to ensure your library's response. If you have any questions, problems, or technical difficulties, please contact The Management Association of Illinois' Survey Department at 800-448-4584.

The ALA-Allied Professional Association continues to work in consultation with the American Library Association Office for Research and Statistics to provide salary data. For a discounted subscription to the database, complete the contact information at the end of the survey and ALA-APA will contact you. For the 25% discount on the price of the report, mention your participation when you place your order with the ALA Store—http://www.alastore.ala.org or 866-746-7252. The Survey will be available in print in the summer of 2010. Contact Jenifer Grady at 800-545-2433, x2424 or jgrady@ala.org for more information.

Sincerely yours,

Keith Michael Fiels
Executive Director, American Library Association-Allied Professional Association

Appendix D. Compensation Surveys Providing Information on Library Workers

Most library salary surveys listed below are conducted on a regular schedule (annual or biennial) and on a regional or national basis. The library literature should be monitored for reports of one-time surveys by individual libraries or associations. Many state library agencies collect salary and benefits data as part of their ongoing statistical gathering efforts from libraries within their own state. There is wide variation, however, in what data are collected and how these are compiled and reported. Most collect only public library data. Academic and school library data may be collected by other state agencies.

In addition, some state and regional library associations collect salary data, issue recommended salary guidelines, set minimum salaries for professional positions or publish reports in association journals or newsletters. As of April 2010, sixteen states had established recommended minimum salaries for public library positions. These include: Connecticut, Illinois, Indiana, Louisiana, Maine, Massachusetts, New Jersey, North Carolina, Ohio, Pennsylvania, Rhode Island, South Carolina, South Dakota, Texas, Vermont, and Wisconsin. Specific dollar amounts are updated regularly by the associations. The latest figures can be found periodically in the classified section of *American Libraries* or *College & Research Libraries News*. These figures are also posted on the ALA-APA website at http://ala-apa.org/improving-salariesstatus/.

A list of state library agency addresses can be found in *The Bowker Annual: Library and Book Trade Almanac* or on the Internet at www.cosla.org under "Member Profiles." Library associations and ALA Chapters can be found in *The Bowker Annual: Library and Book Trade Almanac* or on the Internet at www.ala.org.

Individual libraries will sometimes conduct private surveys of institutions of comparable size or in the same geographical area, either through an outside consulting firm or by calling libraries informally. For the most part, these surveys are not published, although the initiating library will often share results with participating libraries. Some library workers are also conducting surveys that compare their salaries with other industries, professions and occupations within their jurisdiction in an effort to achieve pay equity with positions requiring comparable skills, effort, responsibilities and working conditions.

The American Library Association Policies related to salary issues may be found in the *ALA Handbook of Organization* at www.ala.org/ala/aboutala/governance/handbook.

Academic Libraries

Association of Research Libraries. *ARL Annual Salary Survey.* Washington, D.C.: ARL, 1973-. Updated annually.

The *ARL Annual Salary Survey* annually reports salaries for more than 12,000 professional positions in ARL member libraries. These data are used to determine whether salaries are competitive, equitable across institutions and personal characteristics and keeping up with inflation. The survey also tracks minority representation in ARL US libraries and reports separate data for health sciences and law libraries. Statistics have been collected and published annually since 1980. Information on this survey can be found at www.arl.org/stats/annualsurveys/salary.

Most current ARL publications will be available in their entirety on the ARL Web site and many are also available in print form. To order, use the online form at www.arl.org/resources/pubs/pubsorderform.shtml or contact the ARL Publications Distribution Center, PO Box 531, Annapolis Junction, MD 20701-0531, (fax) 301-206-9789, pubs@arl.org.

College and University Professional Association for Human Resources. *Administrative Compensation Survey (AdComp)*. Knoxville, TN: CUPA-HR. Updated annually.

The survey provides salary and demographic data for senior-level administrative positions. There is also a short Pay Practices section asking about who the CHRO reports to and about "incentive" compensation for selected positions.

For the print edition the cost ranges from $170 to $340; for Data on Demand (online access), from $530 to $1060. Contact CUPA-HR, 1811 Commons Point Dr., Knoxville, TN 37932, 865-637-7673, (fax) 865-637-7674, www.cupahr.org/surveys/order.asp.

College and University Professional Association for Human Resources. *Mid-Level Administrative and Professional Salary Survey (Mid-Level)*. Knoxville, TN: CUPA-HR. Updated annually.

This survey features provides salary and rate structure data for mid-level positions; survey also provides data on pay practices. See contact information above.

Griffiths, Dr. José-Marie, Donald W. King with Songphan Choemprayong. *A National Study of the Future of Academic Librarians in the Workforce*. Winter 2008.

This study, funded by the Institute of Museum and Library Services, reports the results of a series of surveys of academic libraries and librarians, including general trends, estimates of employment demand from 2007 to 2017; staffing patterns, demographics and career patterns; trends in academic library expenditures, services and functions; and implications of librarian training and education.

Public Libraries

American Library Association. Public Library Association. *Public Library Data Service Statistical Report*. Chicago, IL: PLA. Updated annually.

Published annually, the *PLDS* report presents exclusive, timely data from more than 800 public libraries across the United States and Canada on finances, library resources, annual use figures and technology. In addition to these valuable topics, each year's edition contains a special survey highlighting statistics on one service area or topic.

To order the print version ($135 with discounts for ALA and PLA members), use the online form at www.ala.org/pla/publications/plds. To order the PLDS database, now

PLAMetrics, ($200–$300) use the online form at www.plametrics.org/package.php. For more information about the PLDS Statistical Report contact the PLA office at 800-545-2433, ext. 5PLA or pla@ala.org.

Griffiths, Dr. José-Marie, Donald W. King with Songphan Choemprayong. *A National Study of the Future of Public Librarians in the Workforce*. Winter 2008.

This study, funded by the Institute of Museum and Library Services, reports the results of a series of surveys of public libraries and librarians, including general trends, estimates of employment demand from 2007 to 2017; staffing patterns, demographics and career patterns; trends in public library expenditures, services and functions; and implications of librarian training and education.

Moulder, Evelina R. "Salaries of Municipal Officials" in *The Municipal Year Book*. Washington, D.C.: International City/County Management Association. Updated annually.

The Municipal Year Book offers salary survey data for municipal and county officials by population group, geographic region, form of government and metro status. The Municipal Year Book is published in April of each year and includes salary data from the previous year. To order, call 800-745-8780 or purchase online at http://bookstore.icma.org. *The Municipal Year Book* costs $156 for non-members.

School Libraries

Educational Research Service. *National Survey of Salaries and Wages in Public Schools*. Arlington, VA: ERS. Updated annually.

ERS publishes an annual report of salaries for public school personnel, which includes data for school librarians and library clerks. The report covers scheduled salaries for professional personnel and actual salaries paid for professional and support personnel by enrollment group, per pupil expenditure and geographic region. It also includes year-to-year, five-year and ten-year information on trends in public school salaries and wages, with comparisons to the Consumer Price Index for each of these periods.

Available from Editorial Projects in Education, 6935 Arlington Rd., Bethesda, MD 20814, 800-346-1834, www.ers.org/surveyresearch/index.html. The price is $150.

Shontz, Marilyn L. et. al. "The SLJ Spending Survey." *School Library Journal,* New York, NY. Updated periodically.

The survey includes data and tables about library media specialists' years of experience and salaries. *School Library Journal,* 160 Varick St., 11th Fl., New York, NY 10013, 646-380-0700, (fax) 646-380-0756, www.schoollibraryjournal.com.

Specialized Libraries

American Association of Law Libraries. *Biennial Salary Survey and Organizational Characteristics.* Chicago, IL: AALL. Updated biennially.

The report summarizes salary information for law libraries with three sections that cover academic libraries, private firm/corporate libraries and state, court and county libraries. The data is broken out and cross-tabbed by position, region, gender, education, years in current position and years of library experience and membership in AALL.

Contact AALL, 105 W. Adams St., Ste. 3300 Chicago, IL 60603-6225, 312-939-4764 x12, (fax) 312-431-1097, orders@aall.com, www.aallnet.org/products/pub_salary_survey.asp. AALL members may browse the online edition free of charge. The hardcopy is $110 for AALL members, $175 for non-members.

Association of Academic Health Sciences Libraries. *Annual Statistics of Medical School Libraries in the United States and Canada.* Seattle, WA: AAHSLD. Updated annually.

Salaries are provided for director, deputy director, associate director, division head, department head, other librarians and entry-level positions. Besides salary data, the survey asks the respondent for years of experience, gender, FTE supervised, ethnicity and race for each professional library staff member. Minimum, maximum and mean are provided for the positions and arranged by region.

It's available at no cost to members of AAHSL and $500 for nonmembers. To acquire the Annual Statistics, contact AAHSL, www.aahsl.org/mc/page.do?sitePageId=84868.

Medical Library Association. *Hay Group/MLA 2008 Salary Survey.* Chicago: MLA. Updated triennially.

Available in summary format to MLA's members via the Association's website, www.mlanet.org. The summary offers detailed information by job title, geographical area, type of institution and more. Print and PDF versions are available from the MLANet store, www.mlanet.org/order/index.html. The pdf edition is $50 for members, $75 for nonmembers. For more information, contact MLA, 65 E. Wacker Pl., Ste. 1900, Chicago, IL 60601-7298, 312-419-9094.

Special Libraries Association. *SLA Annual Salary Survey.* Alexandria, VA: SLA. Updated annually.

Salaries are reported at the 10th, 25th, 50th (median), 75th and 90th percentiles and contain breakdowns by industry, geographic region, administrative responsibility, sex, education level and experience. Data for the U.S. and Canada are presented in separate tables.

The salary survey is a comprehensive report containing the most accurate U.S. and Canadian salary information gathered by a member survey. A wide variety of variables are covered including industry type, geographical area, job title, budget range and years of experience.

The report is available to SLA members for $65, $125 non-members as a PDF download. Contact Special Libraries Association, 331 S. Patrick St., Alexandria, VA 22314, 703-647-4900, www.sla.org/content/resources/research/salary-surveys/salsur2009/index.cfm.

More Salary Surveys for Other Library Workers and Related Information Professionals

For salary data on other types of workers that may be employed in libraries, the following surveys might be useful:

Abbott, Langer and Associates, Inc.,/ERi Salary Surveys conducts annual or biennial salary surveys for the following fields: legal and related jobs in business and industry; industrial engineers; plant and facilities managers and engineers; consulting engineering firms; consulting firms; independent lab/testing/inspection firms; geologists; human resources/personnel department; service department; nonprofit organizations; research and development; manufacturing; food and beverage processing; security/loss prevention dept.; MIS/data processing; accounting departments; accounting firms; advertising agencies; sales/marketing management; direct marketing; life sciences and telecommunications.

All Nonprofit Organizations. Updated annually.

This report provides pay data on benchmark jobs in nonprofit organizations (including a Director of Information). It reports by type of organization, number of employees, fiscal size, geographic scope of service and location; it also compares each type of organization to each other variable. Online pdf is $689. For more information, contact ERI Salary Surveys, 8575 164th Ave. NE, Ste. 100, Redmond, WA 98052 USA Telephone (877) 210-6563 Fax: (877) 239-2457, survey.sales@erieri.com, http://salary-surveys.erieri.com/.

Grady, Jenifer and Denise Davis. *ALA-APA Salary Survey: Non-MLS—Public and Academic.* Chicago: American Library Association Allied Professional Association. 2007. Updated irregularly.

This survey is a gathering of information on discrete positions within the library that do not require a MLS degree from an ALA-accredited institution. The information is reported for both public and academic libraries. The two library universes are stratified by regions and states for analysis. This publication is $100, $90 to ALA members and is available from the ALA Online Store, 866-Shop ALA, www.alastore.ala.org. For more information about the Non-MLS Salary Survey, contact ALA-APA at lswader@ala.org or call 800-545-2433 x4278.

Library Mosaics was a bi-monthly magazine for support staff in libraries, media and information centers. The last support staff salary survey published by *Library Mosaics* was the "2003 Salary Survey" by Raymond Roney and Charlie Fox in the July/August issue. The magazine collected and reported six support staff salary surveys between 1989 and 2003. It provides a general overview of support staff salaries, salary ceilings and pay equity. For past issues, contact Library Mosaics, Yenor, Inc., PO Box 5171, Culver City, CA 90231, 310-645-4998.

U.S. Department of Labor, Bureau of Labor Statistics, National Compensation Survey program annually produces information on wages by occupation for many metropolitan areas and also for the nation as a whole. It provides data on occupational earnings, employer costs for wages, salaries, benefits and details of employer-provided benefit and establishment practices. This umbrella program combines the Occupational Compensation Surveys, the Employment Cost Index and the Employee Benefits Survey. For more information, phone 202-691-6199 or visit http://stats.bls.gov/ncs/.

Other

Association for Library and Information Science Education. *ALISE Statistical Report and Database.* TN: ALISE, 1980–. Updated annually.

Average and median salaries for faculty and administrators in ALISE member schools are provided in this annual report by sex, rank and term of appointment.

Back issues (1981–) of the report are available from 65 ALISE, E. Wacker Pl., Ste. 1900 Chicago, IL 60601-7246, 312-795-0996, fax: 312-419-8950, contact@alise.org. The surveys from 1997 to 2004 are available for free from http://ils.unc.edu/ALISE/.

College and University Professional Association for Human Resources. *National Faculty Salary Survey by Discipline and Rank in Four-Year Colleges and Universities.* Knoxville, TN: CUPA-HR. Updated annually.

Annual surveys collect data for faculty ranks in disciplines and major fields. Communications, Communication Technologies, Computer Information Sciences and Library Sciences are included. The listings are for those who teach in library science programs, not those who hold faculty rank as academic librarians.

For the print edition the cost ranges from $170 to $340; for Data on Demand (online access), from $530 to $1060. Contact CUPA-HR, 1811 Commons Point Dr., Knoxville, TN 37932, 877-CUPA-HR4 (877-287-2474), 865-637-7673, fax: 865-637-7674, www.cupahr.org/surveys/order.asp.

Griffiths, José-Marie. *Future of Librarians in the Workforce.*

This is a multi-year study sponsored by the Institute for Museum and Library Science (IMLS) that will identify the nature of anticipated labor shortages in the library and information science (LIS) field over the next decade; assess the number and types of library and information science jobs that will become available in the U.S. either through retirement or new job creation; determine the skills that will be required to fill such vacancies; and recommend effective approaches to recruiting and retaining workers to fill them. The study will result in better tools for workforce planning and management, better match of demand and supply, and improved recruitment and retention of librarians. The study is led by Dr. José-Marie Griffiths, Dean of the School of Information and Library Science at the University of North Carolina at Chapel Hill and includes researchers from the University of Pittsburgh, Syracuse University, the Special Libraries Association (SLA), the Association of Research Libraries (ARL), and the American Society for Information Science & Technology (ASIS&T).

See: http://libraryworkforce.org.

French, Jennifer. 2006. *Fast Facts: Salaries of Librarians and Other Professionals Working in Libraries.* ED3/110.10/No. 238. Denver, CO: Library Research Service.

Fast Facts documents the pay distinctions between librarians' salaries in Colorado and other professions' salaries in the state. As well, the report compares all of the professional salaries in Colorado to national averages. The report is from 2006 and is available at www.lrs.org/documents/fastfacts/238_BLS_lib_salaries.pdf.

"Placements and Salaries." *Library Journal.* Updated annually.

An annual survey since 1951 of ALA accredited library and information studies education programs (usually published in the October 15th issue of *Library Journal* with data from previous calendar year). For each reporting school, the low, high, average and median salaries are reported for men, women and total placements. This information is also provided for five regions of the U.S. An additional table shows the distribution of high, low, average and median salaries by type of library for men, women and total placements. The current report is available at www.libraryjournal.com/lj/careers/salaries/887218305/placements__salaries_survey_2010.html.csp.

Employee Benefits

Although some states collect data on employee benefits, little information is collected on a regional or national level on a regular basis for library workers. The last report on Employee Benefits was in the *Librarian Salary Survey* supplemental questions from 2008. The report may be found on the ALA-APA Web site at ala-apa.org/?s=2008+supplemental+questions.

Appendix E. Nonbinding Minimum Salary for Professional Librarians

ENDORSEMENT OF A NONBINDING MINIMUM SALARY FOR PROFESSIONAL LIBRARIANS

WHEREAS, The among the stated goals of the Allied Professional Association is "Direct support of comparable worth and pay equity initiatives, and other activities designed to improve the salaries and status of librarians and other library workers;"[1] and

WHEREAS, The Mean Librarian Salary in 2006 was $56,259;[2] and

WHEREAS, Over three-quarters of respondent library workers support the establishment of salary minimums for librarians, with the commonest salary figure cited being $40,000;[3] and

WHEREAS, The National Education Association has established a minimum salary of at least $40,000 for public school teachers, professionals whose qualifications closely mirror those of librarians,[4] now, be it

RESOLVED, that the American Library Association-Allied Professional Association endorses a minimum salary for professional librarians of not less than $40,000 per year; and, be it further

RESOLVED, that the details of this endorsement shall be published and otherwise disseminated by the Director of the ALA Allied Professional Association as appropriate.

Mover: Michael McGrorty, Councilor at Large
Seconder: Rob Banks, Kansas Chapter Councilor

2009 Update—$42,181/year for professional librarians, and $13.52/hour for library employees.

Council Actions

During the American Library Association 2007 Midwinter Meeting in Seattle, WA, on January 22, 2007, the ALA-APA Council took the following actions:

Voted, To adopt APACD #15, Endorsement of a Nonbinding Minimum Salary for Professional Librarians.

---

1. See www.ala-apa.org/about/about.html.
2. See "Librarian Salary Survey Reports Mean Librarian Salary Up More Than 4% to $56,259 in 2006" available at www.ala-apa.org/newsletter/vol3no11/salaries.htm.
3. As found in the attached Survey.
4. See *Professional Pay: about NEA's Salary Initiative* at www.nea.org/pay/about.html.